The Songs of Blind Folk

CORpoRealities: Discourses of Disability

David T. Mitchell and Sharon L. Snyder, editors

The Songs of Blind Folk

*African American Musicians and the
Cultures of Blindness*

Terry Rowden

THE UNIVERSITY OF MICHIGAN PRESS
Ann Arbor

Copyright © by the University of Michigan 2009
All rights reserved
Published in the United States of America by
The University of Michigan Press
Manufactured in the United States of America
♾ Printed on acid-free paper

2012   2011   2010   2009   4   3   2   1

A CIP catalog record for this book is available from the British Library.

Library of Congress Cataloging-in-Publication Data

Rowden, Terry.
    The songs of blind folk : African American musicians and the
cultures of blindness / Terry Rowden.
       p.   cm. — (Corporealities. Discourses of disability)
    Includes bibliographical references and index.
    ISBN-13: 978-0-472-07064-0 (cloth : alk. paper)
    ISBN-10: 0-472-07064-9 (cloth : alk. paper)
    ISBN-13: 978-0-472-05064-2 (pbk. : alk. paper)
    ISBN-10: 0-472-05064-8 (pbk. : alk. paper)
    1. African Americans—Music—History and criticism.   2. African
American musicians.   3. Blind musicians.   I. Title.
ML3556.R68   2009
780.87'10973—dc22   2009014542

for My Mother
Lueretha Mixon
❧
and My Aunts
Ida Mae Robinson
and Erma Cook

Acknowledgments

It is a pleasure to acknowledge the support this project has received over the years. I am especially appreciative of the support through grants and release time that I received from The College of Wooster during my happy tenure there and of the efforts of LeAnn Fields, Marcia LaBrenz, and the editorial and production staff at the University of Michigan Press.

Over the years many friends and colleagues have offered either formal or informal comments or suggestions concerning this project. Thomas Prendergast and Maria Teresa Micaela Prendergast provided intellectual and personal support in more ways than they may have imagined. I would also like to thank Brenda Allen, Martha J. Cutter, Janice Cook Johnson, Jane Garrity, Sidney Goldfarb, Joanne Frye, Nancy Grace, Peter Havholm, Karen Jacobs, Byron Mayes, Peter Pozefsky, Attilio Rezzonico, Debra Shostak, Thomas Tierney, and Christina Tortora.

I am particularly indebted to Kari Winter, who provides me with an image of personal and intellectual integrity by which I never failed to be inspired; and to Elizabeth Ezra, whose two decades of intellectual friendship could not be fully acknowledged in anything less than a book-length manuscript.

ᥕᑋ

Finally, I want to thank my partner, Rick Wells, for his many years of unstinting support and encouragement.

Contents

Introduction

It is only in his music, which Americans are able to admire because a protective sentimentality limits their understanding of it, that the Negro in America has been able to tell his story.
—James Baldwin, "Many Thousands Gone"

The stories of blind and visually impaired African American musicians have mirrored the changes in America's image of African Americans and the social possibilities of the black community over the last 150 years.[1] By looking closely we can discover how, for these musicians and the audiences who have sought them out, their blindness, like their blackness, has been a "difference that has made a difference" in both the music they produced and the ways that music has been received.[2]

The sentimentality that James Baldwin pinpointed as a component of the cultural narratives of black Americans has played an even greater role in the reception of artists who are both black and blind. For the most part, however, blindness as a disability or even as a distinctive physical condition has not been sensitively or consistently factored into critical assessments of even the most celebrated African American blind artists. They are as much black people as they are blind people, and the converse is also true: the blind person of African American descent is just as urgently and dynamically a blind black child, a blind black man, or a blind black woman. The particular types of recognition, denigration, and acclaim that blind African Americans have received are very different than for their white counterparts. By focusing on the changing receptions that performers as varied as Blind Lemon Jefferson, Arizona Dranes, the Blind Boys of Alabama, Art Tatum, and Stevie Wonder have received, this book hopes to shed light on a network of interrelated identity concerns that might initially seem to be unrelated political and social issues. Any consideration of these men and women who happened to be black and blind (and much more) needs to actively factor in race and gender in unprecedented ways.

Blind people have distinguished themselves across all forms of African American music (with the important exceptions of rap and hip-hop), while comparatively fewer blind white artists have achieved popular recognition. The emergence of new types of blind black musicianship over time has starkly revealed the life possibilities of African Americans at various cultural moments. While linked by their blindness, these performers are also distinct individuals uniquely shaped by differing backgrounds and the particular musical forms to which they were exposed. Their individual lives reflect the changing conditions of American life as they have impacted all African Americans and reveal the possibilities for social recognition, personal agency, and economic survival that those changes both generated and nullified. In fact, it is their distinctiveness as performers, rather than their similarities as blind people enacting an unchanging and unraced experience of "blindness," that will become most apparent as we consider their lives and careers.

As a means of expressing African American group consciousness, black music, perhaps more than any other art form, has functioned as a "cultural site"—sociologist Jon Cruz's term for "an intersection where we see social interests and social struggles coincide and entwine."[3] If we consider blindness as a cultural site (rather than as a more or less incidental personal characteristic or an experientially stable social identity), we can recognize that the ways in which we talk about blindness or refuse to talk about it are determined by the ways we talk or refuse to talk about a range of other issues. These words and silences have established the parameters within which the personal agency and particular creations of blind African American performers have been understood by both blind people and the sighted.[4] Upon closer examination, an image of the music of blind African Americans emerges as something that cannot be tidily assigned to a notion of black expressivity as such or, on the other hand, sentimentally excised from it as being "different."

Although we must be wary of the tendency to endow blind people as a group with special characteristics, it's clear that many blind individuals have out of sheer necessity achieved prodigious development in the area of music performance. For centuries, music has been one of the few respectable careers available for the blind (as it was for African Americans). This factor perhaps helps to explain the prevalence of prodigies (or at least of performers presented to the public as prodigies) among the ranks of blind musicians. The special conditions of African Americans over the more than one hundred years since the emergence of the nineteenth-century musical phenomenon Blind Tom Bethune have in fact produced a number of blind black virtuosos. While many blind people have been recognized for their significant contributions to society, for most of its recorded history, blindness has been more closely linked with poverty— not prodigious achievement or financial success.[5] Considering the historically strong correlation between blackness and economic deprivation, it's not surprising that blind African Americans have been unusually prominent in American musical culture. During the first four decades of the twentieth century, the United States provided a few segregated and underfunded vocational "blind schools" that taught blind people the most basic of job skills, without significantly ameliorating or even acknowledging the almost epidemic levels of blindness among African Americans, caused by poverty, accidents, and a range of treatable but untreated illnesses and medical conditions. This policy of neglect was particularly evident in the Southern states, where most African Americans lived. Frances Koestler has written about services for the black blind during this period:

> As was generally the case with all types of segregated schools, the educational facilities offered Negro children who were blind were inferior. A 1939 Foundation survey revealed that some of the schools for blind black children had to make do with hand-me-downs from their sister schools for blind white children, not merely in the form of worn furniture, chipped crockery, and threadbare towels, but also in classroom materials such as Braille books whose dots were so worn down as to be all but indistinguishable.[6]

It is hard to imagine a more striking symbol of social disenfranchisement than the worn-down and therefore unreadable dots of an overused Braille primer. Such an image does, however, highlight the fact that, then as now, economic privilege has fundamentally determined the extent to which a given disabled individual has been able to acquire the basic skills that could expand his or her range and possibilities. The double consciousness that W. E. B. Du Bois recognized as an essential component of African American subjectivity and the double disenfranchisement that has been a component of black women's experience of Americanness are magnified further when the condition of a disability is also present. The intersecting experiences of oppression that help explain the presence and particularity of blind black performers fundamentally negated their ability to live their lives as "simply" black or "simply" blind or, more drastically, "simply" American, even if that was something to which a particular person may have aspired. As disability studies scholar Petra Kuppers insists, "No study should discuss disability performance without acknowledging the history of oppression that had for so long kept disabled performers away from the 'aesthetic' stage and inducements of prestige, potential careers, and professional lives."[7]

If blind people could play such a significant role in the world of African American music, this is to a great extent because there were simply so many of them, while relatively few social resources were available to help them achieve independent adult lives—or even survive. The excessive rates of blindness in the black community and the impoverished conditions that generated them reflected the disproportionately negative medical and educational environment that African Americans have faced throughout history. Helen Keller, one of this country's most acute observers of social inequity, was particularly sensitive to the plight of the black blind, whom she called "the hardest pressed and the least cared-for among my blind fellows." Keller wrote of their condition:

> In my travels up and down the continent I have visited their shabby school buildings and witnessed their pathetic struggle against want. I have been shocked by the meagreness of their education, lack of proper medical care, and the discrimination which limits their employment chances. I feel it a disgrace that in this great wealthy land such injustice should exist to men and women of a different race— and blind at that.[8]

Across the country, the condition of the black blind was more severe than that of their white counterparts, but because more African Americans lived in the South, their problems in that region were more pressing and their attempts to solve them more varied and culturally visible. It is not surprising then that in the Jim Crow South, the structural inequality to which African Americans were subjected could generate and sustain scores of blind bluesmen and street singers and the gospel groups of "Blind Boys" who would leave an indelible imprint on blues and gospel music.

The ability of blind performers across all ethnic groups to achieve and maintain successful careers as singers and musicians has generally depended on the willingness of audiences to accord them a comprehensible role in one of the standard narratives of blindness as "difference." These narratives reflect the social constructionist position on disability, in which, Henri-Jacques Stiker argues, "There is no disability, no disabled, outside precise social and cultural constructions; there is no attitude toward disability outside a series of societal references and constructs."[9] This perspective enables us to recognize the extent to which the particular construction of black musical artists as worth hearing and seeing has also reflected "the intertwined historical background of blacks as physical curiosities and blacks as entertainers."[10] Hopefully, consideration of the ways that respect for blind and other disabled performers as heroes or "wonders" can devolve into covert forms of disrespect for them as "freaks" will complicate our tendencies to uncritically view these performers as members of any of these groups.

In his controversial and hugely influential book *The Making of Blind Men,* Robert A. Scott theorizes that "blindness is a social role that people who have serious difficulty seeing or who cannot see at all must learn how to play."[11] According to Scott, "The various attitudes and patterns of behavior that characterize people who are blind are not inherent in their condition but, rather, are acquired through ordinary processes of social learning."[12] Close consideration of prominent blind African American performers and lesser-known figures reveals the ways in which the blindness role as enacted by these artists has been reconfigured as opportunities for both blind people and blacks have changed. Throughout history, blind African Americans have been molded by the same forces as other blacks, but for blind performers it has been the production of some sellable image of normality, not the exoticizing of their "difference" as blind people, that has characterized their relations with their overwhelmingly sighted audiences. Blind people often find themselves in the position of having to establish for the sighted what they themselves take for granted: their normality.

When considering how blindness has affected or determined the life chances of blind musical artists, it is important to keep in mind Frances Koestler's statement that "the conditions commonly subsumed under the heading of blindness actually fall into three categories: total blindness, legal blindness, and functional blindness."[13] The general failure of the sighted to recognize these distinctions becomes clear when one realizes how great a range of degrees and types of visual impairment characterize those individuals who have been assigned to the category of "the blind." These differences have been generated by a number of factors:

they include "variable definitions of blindness, unreliable eye examinations, the reluctance of some physicians, families, and subjects to report blindness, and an occasional lack of awareness of the presence of blindness in an individual."[14] Regardless of these variables, throughout history, "the areas with the highest prevalence rates also have [had] the highest percentage of non-white population."[15] The ability of blind performers to consistently establish and maintain their identities and popularity as performers has been complicated by the fact that the response to blindness can vary across national, ethnic, and class lines. The emergence of blind performers like the Malian couple Amadou Bagayoko and Mariam Doumbia into real prominence as culturally representative figures may reflect their origins in the so-called developing world, where blindness is still relatively common.[16]

From both sides of the black/white racial divide that has too often been presented as the "truth" of American race relations, both celebratory and denigrating accounts of the black body have a long and ideologically charged history. Many aspects of the lives of blind African American musicians and singers have been representative of the lives of both African Americans and the disabled, as members of these groups have attempted to make their way in the simultaneously racist and ableist public sphere(s) of American life. As public figures, blind performers must be read in relation to both the aural and the visual identities they create as individuals and the cultural expectations that make a particular identity readable or unreadable, entertaining or disturbing, at a particular historical moment for a particular individual or group. Over the span of the more than 150 years covered in this book, cultural context, more than anything specific to blindness itself, has determined whether a particular blind performer has been positioned as a freak, a prodigy, a genius, or—far less frequently—a more or less ordinary person making the best of a difficult but neither tragic nor dehumanizing physical condition.[17]

Chief among the categories that demarcate degrees of visual impairment is the difference between congenital and adventitious blindness: "A person who was born without sight is *congenitally blind,* while one who lost his or her sight at some later time is said to be *adventitiously blinded.*"[18] Many observers have failed to recognize such distinctions, and this has led to their frequent misreadings of displays of confident physical mobility, social agency, and emotional well-being by particular blind musicians. These misreadings have generated both the excessive praise and the misguided sympathy to which blind performers have responded with varying degrees of acceptance, contestation, and subversion.

It is telling that almost all of the musical performers who have achieved significant popular success have been either congenitally blind or visually impaired from a very young age.[19] One of the reasons may be that for the congenitally blind, musical instruments have a relatively stronger appeal, perhaps functioning as what the psychologist D. W. Winnecott called "transitional objects." These are "those objects the infants used to appropriate into their experiences the 'not-me-ness' of the world and to quell the attendant anxiety of this experience," while growing into psychological and social maturity.[20] Perhaps the regularity of the effects that can be produced by a musical instrument serves to lessen the anxiety produced by a world that for a congenitally blind child must seem even more unpredictable and threatening, for a significantly longer time, than it does for the once sighted.

While a number of blind African American musical artists have achieved success and visibility, their conditions have rarely been linked to those of other blind people, a fact that may demonstrate the special symbolic force of blindness as a disability. As an image of functional incapacity, the inability to see engenders a particularly high degree of anxiety for the visually unimpaired. It certainly generates more anxiety than deafness seems to for the hearing. Given this resistance by the sighted to engage emotionally with blindness as a positively livable condition, it is perhaps not surprising that so little specific consideration has been given to these artists as "blind people" or, more generally, "people with disabilities." Admirers and critical readers have consistently refused to consider the blindness of blind musicians and singers as essentially the same as the blindness of the person with the white cane whom one sees on the subway making his way home. When the artists' blindness is addressed, it is usually as a human-interest sidebar to a consideration of "the only thing that really matters," their music. For instance, few of even their most devoted fans have any knowledge of the causes of the blindness of such legendary performers as Blind Willie Johnson, Ray Charles, or Rahsaan Roland Kirk. Instead the achievements of these men have more often been read as either miraculously uninfluenced by their inability to see or as exceptionally remarkable precisely because of it. The lives and careers of blind performers provide innumerable examples of how encounters with blind people can generate narratives in which acts considered unexceptional when performed by a sighted individual are read as evidencing prodigious or even supernatural talent when performed by a blind person.

Deborah Marks suggests that "homogeneous patterns among the blind population only emerge because of the way in which blind people are stigmatised and placed in positions of dependence in relation to the seeing population."[21] Accordingly, because of the particular difficulties that blind people have had in establishing strong forms of communal identity and articulating a sense of group consciousness, attempts to reveal the particulars of blindness as a condition that is lived in many of the same ways by a wide range of people have been much more sporadic than those accorded other disabilities such as deafness. In *From Homer to Helen Keller: A Social and Educational Study of the Blind,* one of the first and most influential considerations of "the blind" as a group, Richard Slayton French opens with the provocative gesture of informing his readers that "there is first of all no 'blind as a class,' and to speak of blind people as such is to miss at the start one of the most fundamental characteristics of the group—their outstanding and sometimes overweening individualism."[22]

The inability of blind people to achieve recognition as a minority group as such underscores the often-made assertion that, unlike for the deaf, "the issue of culture identification is not generally raised by blind persons."[23] Alternatively, it is a disability studies commonplace that "the Deaf" consist of "that group of deaf people who define themselves or are defined by others as having a minority group status based on their linguistic and cultural difference, and who distance themselves from notions of deafness as hearing impairment and disability."[24] Extrapolating from the notion that there is no blind obvious analogue to the state of "attitudinal deafness" that characterizes deaf culture, we can see research on blindness as having been either stymied or liberated, depending on one's point of view.[25] As with the many studies that have preceded it, this book does not seek to identify any consistently distinguishing set of psychological perspectives or linguistic markers that can be used to ground notions of an expressive or emotional economy that is unique to the blind.

Unlike the deaf, the blind have to a great extent not recognized each other because, more than may initially seem evident, such recognition may be tied to the ability to see and be seen. The blind lack the expressive immediacy of sign language, which has made community formation among the deaf so successful, or any such "signage," preventing blind people from establishing comparable levels of communal recognition and empowerment. For instance, it is not hard to imagine a scene in which two blind people could find themselves sitting across from each other in a library reading the same book in Braille while being completely unaware of each other's existence.

Some observers have even suggested that sensitivity demands that we reject the idea that there is a social entity that can be accurately referred to as "the blind." They have argued that "the expression 'the blind' . . . gives the impression that blindness is the only important characteristic of visually impaired people."[26] While one should be mindful of this possibility, avoiding terms like "the blind" or, even more generally, "the disabled" can just as easily lead to counterproductive types of euphemistic "beating around the bush." While recognizing that there are no people who are "just" blind, we must also remember that there are people who "are" blind and that in most areas of their lives that "difference does make a difference." in ways of which we should be aware and respectful.[27]

From an activist standpoint, the desire to maintain recognition of blind people as individuals with varied histories and degrees of impairment must, as it has with African Americans, coexist with a commitment to achieving the social objectives that only some sense of group identity can provide. This book employs the term "the blind," rather than the more general "blind people," not because visual impairment is the only important characteristic of the individuals being discussed, but because their impairment and its potentially transpersonal consequences are the aspects being scrutinized. In most cases, these are moments when I attempt to read a particular performer's blindness into a narrative constructed to divert attention away from the particularity of his or her enactment of the role of "blind person" or from some disturbing aspects of his or her reality as one.

Recognition of an individual's performance of the blind role is often complicated by the continuities that categorize blind people, however tenuously, as a people about whom comprehensible "group" statements can be made. Much the same could be said for the group identity of African Americans. It is this overlap that provides the basis for a cross-reading of the blind black musical performer in relation to the cultures of both disability and black America. Although as a social construct, the group identity of African Americans has been more historically accessible and narratively straightforward than that of the blind, the ability to productively position themselves as black while blind has consistently characterized the most successful blind African American performers.

For instance, the dynamics of the blind role as it intersects with African American identity are beautifully expressed in Lynn Manning's poem "The Magic Wand":

> Quick-change artist extraordinaire,
> I whip out my folded cane
> and change from black man to blind man
> with a flick of my wrist.
> It is a profound metamorphosis—
> From God gifted wizard of groundball
> dominating backboards across America,
> To God-gifted idiot savant
> pounding out chart-busters on a cock-eyed whim;
> From sociopathic gang-banger with death for eyes
> To all seeing soul with saintly spirit;
> From rape deranged misogynist
> to poor motherless child;
> From welfare-rich pimp
> to disability-rich gimp;
> And from "White man's burden"
> to every man's burden.
>
> It is always a profound metamorphosis.
> Whether from cursed by man to cursed by God
> or from scripture condemned to God ordained,
> my final form is never of my choosing.
> I only wield the wand;
> You are the magician.[28]

The works of blind musicians and singers are rarely read as self-conscious examples of this kind of "disability art."[29] This may be because they are performers in popular forms, and thus the possibility for them to see their music-making as primarily a form of self-expression has always been tempered by their realization of the economic necessity of attracting and entertaining sighted audiences. Like all disabilities, blindness is always caused by "something," and that "something" is almost by definition "something" that the sighted would rather not dwell upon when they are trying to have a good time. To a great extent, this potential for producing "dis-ease" no doubt accounts for the general lack of extended and especially negative references to blindness that we find in the work of most blind performers.

The ability to which a particular blind performer can interpret and control the response of people whom they cannot visually "read" ultimately determines their long-term success or failure. The necessity of controlling the responses of unseen audiences makes the ability to normalize oneself, and thereby create the space in which "entertainment" can take place, a more self-conscious and labor-intensive enterprise for a blind entertainer than it ever is for a sighted one. A musical performer on stage becomes an object for both aural and visual consumption, and few people consume anything unless they believe that its effects will be pleasurable, salubrious, or at least benign. Even sighted critics, drawn to a particular blind performer by a desire to provide validation of his or her work, have usually been reluctant in their narratives of appreciation to provide the specifying details that would give blindness any kind of explanatory prominence.

Unfortunately, these validating efforts are often filtered through stereotyping narratives that the sighted unwittingly invoke in their attempts to imagine the social and personal subjectivity of the blind. Therefore, it is important that we be actively aware of what Donald Kirtley calls the "three major stereotypes of the blind in American culture: (1) 'the blind beggar'; (2) 'the blind genius'; and (3) 'the superstition of sensory compensation.'"[30] The extent to which the culture has used these stereotypes as the primary lens for viewing blind people has changed over time, as its ability to engage with disability and physical difference has changed. Still, as I will show, there have been few periods in which each of these stereotypes has not played a major role in determining the ease or difficulty with which blind people have been able to establish and maintain successful and fulfilling lives and careers.

No role has been more strongly linked to disability than musicianship has to blindness. The idea of the special aptitude of blind people for music has been all but taken for granted since the beginning of organized education of the blind. Hector Chevigny and Sydell Braverman note of Valentin Haüy, who established L'Institution Nationale des Jeunes Aveugles (The National Institution for Young Blind People) — the first known school for the blind — in Paris in 1784: "He seems to have believed that all the blind are more than usually gifted musically, a belief shared by his successors in the directorship of the school. In subsequent years, noted one observer, it became little more than a sort of national conservatory of music for the blind."[31] This truncation of the pedagogical and occupational options available to blind people occurred despite the fact that, as Richard Slayton French puts it, expressing a point that has been thoroughly established by subsequent research, "blindness in itself gives no right of eminent domain in the realm of music any more than deafness implies talent in drawing or modeling."[32] Still, it has been the visibility of blind musicians and singers over millennia that has given music-making its exemplary status as "the thing that blind people can do."

The image of the beggar has long been associated with a variety of disabling conditions, but it is especially entrenched with blind people, who have historically been viewed as people incapable of supporting themselves. The dispossessed, blind or otherwise, have long recognized that nothing facilitates successful street-corner importuning as much as the display of musical talent. It is as a counternarrative to this idea that a blind man on a corner singing for change is, to quote Spike Lee, "doing the right thing" that the notion of the inherent musicality of blind people may have evolved. The possibility that an individual could be deprived of something so apparently fundamental as sight and be given nothing in return offends our basic sense of cosmic justice. When these elements are brought together, the fact that the African American community would generate such high numbers of blind performers becomes as socially unexceptional as is the fact that a racially biased culture produces high numbers of black prisoners. In fact, the entire culture of blind blues musicians was enabled by the establishment of the street corner and the tin cup as indicatively appropriate places and tools for the performance of blind black male identity.

Even the most apparently affirmative stereotype generated by notions of blind musicality, that of the blind genius, has not served blind people well. If, as Mihaly Csikszentmihalyi suggests, "it is impossible to be a genius . . . in the absence of a symbolic system," the symbolic system that grounds the notion of the blind genius, despite its seemingly positive potential, only serves to denaturalize blindness as a simply physical event and to strengthen the "ableist" presumptions that position blind people as "other."[33] Simi Linton points out that "ableism also includes the idea that a person's abilities or characteristics are determined by disability."[34] Although the number of blind people who have managed to support themselves as musicians has never been as great as myth would have it, in recent years the widening of opportunities for blind people has coincided with other social processes to lessen the number of blind musical performers even more.[35] This reduction has been especially apparent in Western countries, where blindness itself is becoming more of a rarity.

In the prevention of blindness, an ounce of prevention is worth considerably more than a pound of cure, and preventative measures that were once available to only a small fraction of the world's population are, at least in the West, now accessible to a much broader range of people. In fact, the rate of registered blindness in technologically advanced societies is now no more than two in every thousand persons.[36] As a consequence of technological advancement, the decline in the rates of blindness, especially as they relate to people of color, reflects the fact that throughout history, blindness, more than any other type of disability, has been "iatrogenically" or medically induced.[37] While seeming oxymoronic, medically induced blindness is functionally congenital in that for the blind child, it naturalizes from birth a condition that is in fact not natural but man- (or woman-) made. The increased professionalization of the practice of medicine and the decline in medically induced blindness in babies and young children in the last century has decreased the number of blind musicians worldwide. Although the world of professional music is populated by performers of all ages, the actual work of becoming a musician is generally a young person's game.

Mainstream audiences have found the sexuality of adult blind musicians more difficult than any other factor in engaging with their performances. The appeal of any disability to the unimpaired can be diminished when the notion of the sexuality of the disabled enters the picture. A reluctance to position the impaired body as sexually attractive reflects ever-narrowing, conventionalized notions of physical attractiveness as primary components of the image-making machine throughout global popular culture. In a media world in which a few extra pounds are often enough to destabilize the star status of both female and male performers, it is not surprising that images of genuine disability can only be brought to light under the signs of sentimentality or monstrosity. In mainstream entertainment, the range of acceptably attractive bodies has become so narrow that blind people are now rarely given the chance to occupy even the small corner of the world stage that they managed to colonize just a few short decades ago. It is with a sense of both the dangers and the pleasures that this enterprise entails that I will attempt to shine a light on this small corner in *The Songs of Blind Folk*.[38]

CHAPTER I

Blind Tom and the
Cultural Politics of Visibility

When considering the lives and music of blind African Americans, the story begins essentially with the blind and mentally impaired slave and piano prodigy who has become known to history as Blind Tom Bethune. As he is simultaneously readable as a "freak," a "genius," an "idiot," and a "victim," much of Tom's appeal could be attributed to the fact that for the tens of thousands who would see him over the course of his career, he functioned as a living representation of the complexities of nineteenth-century America's cultural and political engagement with issues of racial and physical difference. After the Civil War, Tom's life and the particulars of his public reception exemplified the conditions not only of the now free African Americans as they attempted to rewrite the narratives that had been used to justify their enslavement but also of a large percentage of the disabled, who found themselves entangled in the webs of sentimentality and "freakery" that dominated the public culture of the period.

The positioning of the disabled as "freaks" served a myriad of purposes in nineteenth-century America. Although Tom was not himself a freak show performer, his importance for late nineteenth-century issues of race and disability was made particularly obvious by the extent to which, from the start, his career was shaped by the dynamics of "freakery." Robert Bogdan, in his classic study, describes the "freak show" phenomenon: "Although freak shows are now on the contemptible fringe, from approximately 1840 through 1940 the formally organized exhibition for amusement and profit of people with physical, mental, or behavioral anomalies, both alleged and real was an accepted part of American life."[1] While it is true that freak shows remained an accepted

Blind Tom Greene Bethune, 1849–1908.
Courtesy New York Library for the Performing Arts.

component of American popular culture well into the twentieth century, it was in the nineteenth century that they achieved their greatest
cultural prominence and most widespread mainstream appeal.[2]

Therefore, it is not surprising that for more than five decades, as a disabled black man Tom Wiggins Bethune could with relatively little negative comment by contemporary observers be subjected to forms of servitude and denigration that seemed all but natural in relation to established

notions of both racial and physical difference. Benjamin Reiss points out that in the nineteenth century, "'freaks' of all races . . . were often under a system of control by their exhibitors so absolute as to approach slavery, and they were certainly not free to protest the conditions of their labor in public."[3] This willingness to exploit the bodies of people with disabilities was made possible by the fact that in nineteenth-century America, disability had not become a part of the culture's conceptual framework as a condition deserving any sustained positive recognition. In fact, according to Gerald N. Grob, "In the late nineteenth century the concept of disability was virtually nonexistent."[4]

After the Civil War, in the wake of a slave society in which racialized and physicalized notions of use value had been legally established as the basis for social recognition and civil rights, the disabled often found themselves relegated to points well beyond the margins of consistently ameliorative concern. This marginalization was even greater for those individuals like Tom who were both disabled and "colored." In its absolute moral divisiveness, slavery had prevented nineteenth-century America from establishing an ethical consensus that could operate across racial lines. Rachel Adams notes, "Those most anxious about their own status as citizens applauded the reassuring vision of nonwhite bodies that absolutely could not be assimilated."[5] In the light of these anxieties, figures of seemingly minuscule cultural significance took on major symbolic weight in white America's attempt to forge a new social contract that could both contain and disenfranchise blacks as citizens. The project of emotional and political reunification that white America undertook after the Civil War required a precise calculation of where the lines of humanity, citizenship, and social agency should be drawn.[6]

As evidenced by the spread of Social Darwinist ideas, the rapid codification of racially discriminatory laws and practices, and the explosion of freak shows into unprecedented prominence, it was the spectacularization of the physically other that arguably made it possible for "normal" and able-bodied white Americans to reestablish a sense of cultural and emotional unity in the period immediately after the Civil War. Linda Frost argues that "freak presentation, because of its emphasis on and exploitation of racial, ethnic, and cultural differences, reaffirmed white audience members' notions of who belonged to the civilized community of the United States by virtue of putting on stage those who did not."[7]

In the categorizing work that took on special urgency after the war, the proliferation of new terms for supposedly substandard individuals became a major growth industry in the social sciences. One of the first groups to be recognized—or, less charitably, formed—by these new classificatory schemas was that composed of those mentally impaired individuals who would come to be known as "idiots."[8]

Given the general cultural resistance to seeing the disabled body as different but still intact and socially worthy, there are few figures who complicate our ability to imagine a positive relationship between agency and difference more decisively than those individuals who, problematically, have been called "idiot savants."[9] Despite its unpleasantness to modern ears, the term "idiot savant," in its oxymoronic explicitness, perfectly reflects the elements of freakishness and fascination that sustained public interest in Blind Tom for almost half a century.[10] In fact, just as Tom did for nineteenth-century audiences, savants and prodigies even today destabilize our ability to imagine an essential relationship between rational self-consciousness and the highest forms of intellectual and artistic achievement. Mentally impaired savants like Tom force us to speculate about the thwarted possibilities that might exist in even the most immature or seemingly aberrant mind or behind the most manifestly "abnormal" exterior.[11]

Tom Wiggins was born on a plantation near Columbus, Georgia, on 25 May 1849 as the twelfth or the fourteenth child (accounts vary) of a slave woman named Charity Greene and a field slave named Domingo Wiggins.[12] In 1850, the blind and, in terms of potential labor value, seemingly worthless child was sold as an "add-on" to the purchase of his parents by Colonel James Bethune of Columbus. Although there was some speculation that Tom may have had limited vision, most accounts make it clear that, if not completely blind, he was without any functionally usable sight. At best, he may simply have had the ability to distinguish light from dark. Within a few years, it became apparent that not only was Tom blind, but he was also, using the contemporary term, "feeble-minded." For the Bethunes, the emergence of this unexpected deficit meant that even the minimal use value that the boy might have had as a blind slave in a world in which blindness was not a particularly uncommon condition among either blacks or whites would not be available to them. Still, in keeping with their sense of themselves as "good" slaveholders, recognition of Tom's "unsoundness" led the Bethune family to accept the fact that he would never be more than a kind of human pet.[13] Before long, however, the Bethunes' "enlightened" attitude would reap huge benefits for the family. Estimates of the amount of money that the family earned from Tom's performances in the United States and Europe range from $50,000 to $100,000 per year; over the years of their "ownership" of him, they may have earned more than $750,000 dollars.

Stories about the emergence of Tom's musical talent vary in their particulars, as the Bethunes disseminated and embellished the narrative over the years. Common to the many accounts, however, is a dramatic scenario in which, by the age of four, with no prompting or instruction, Tom had begun to play the piano with a degree of proficiency that in the light of both his age and his disabilities seemed practically supernatural. More reasonably, however, Tom's sudden proficiency, combined with the basic predisposition for musical performance that by definition characterizes musical savants, reveals a particularly striking example of what Russell Sanjek calls "that process of eavesdropping that had permitted slaves to become familiar with the white man's music since the summer of 1619."[14] When read in relation to both the specific dynamics of savantism and the interracial domestic relations of the antebellum South, not only is Tom's proficiency less surprising, but it becomes clear that its expression through the piano was itself generated by the particulars of nineteenth-century musical culture and its notions of genteel domesticity. Leon Plantinga points out that in the nineteenth century, "music was woven into the very fabric of social interaction; it was part of the system of signs by which people communicated with each other. And for the entire century this occurred routinely around that familiar fixed object, symbol of both success and sensibility: the piano."[15] Correlatively, the widespread availability of pianos in nineteenth-century American homes contributed to the plethora of piano prodigies that the culture produced.

Not surprisingly, in a world in which the piano signified so much, Colonel Bethune moved quickly to capitalize on the commercial potential of his strange property.[16] After a few generally unsuccessful efforts at formal instruction, Bethune provided training for Tom by hiring musicians to play in his presence, assuming, correctly, that the preternaturally receptive boy would simply absorb their pieces into his growing repertoire. By the age of six, Tom was improvising and creating original compositions, and at eight he was performing in public. Soon Bethune hired a manager, Perry Oliver, to oversee the boy's life on the road and to orchestrate a performance schedule that often required as many as four concerts per day. In the early years of his career, Bethune and Oliver restricted Tom's performances to the South or to Northern audiences friendly to slavery for fear that Tom's story would be used by abolitionists to further the cause of black freedom or, later, that he would be spirited away from them by post-Emancipation forces.

Without doubt, the Bethune family's control of Tom was made easier by the particular ways in which his talent and his impairments were read by the media of nineteenth-century America. For instance, reflecting the construction of Tom as a "marvelous" but essentially freakish performer, an advertisement for one of his earliest appearances at Armory Hall in New Orleans in 1861 presented him as

> the wonder of the World—The Marvel of the Age—The Greatest living musician—only ten years old, and Master of the piano—playing two pieces of music at once and conversing at the same time—performing with his back to the instrument. . . . He will also play the secondo or bass to any one from the audience, without ever having heard it before, and will then change seats and play the primo.[17]

Although interest in Tom would wax and wane over the years, the peak of his public recognition occurred in 1860, when he gave a command performance at the White House before President James Buchanan. Reports of this performance, coupled with a widely read article by Rebecca Harding Davis published in the *Atlantic Monthly* two years later, soon made him one of the most popular and lucrative concert attractions of his day.

In the context of the period's anxieties about race and the "Race Problem," represented by the looming prospect of black freedom, the impact of Davis's article, which contributed so greatly to Tom's success, is not hard to fathom. In what would become the single most read piece about him to appear during his life, Davis constructed an image of Tom, as both a person and a performer, in which the elements of appreciation and denigration are so tightly interwoven that both the pro- and the anti-Tom factions could find ample evidence to support their preconceptions. In the type of language that would later be reproduced by many of her contemporaries with varying degrees of sympathy and animus, Davis informed her readers that

> in the every-day apparent intellect, in reason or judgment, he is but one degree above an idiot,—incapable of comprehending the simplest conversation on ordinary topics, amused or enraged with

trifles such as would affect a child of three years old. On the other side, his affections are alive, even vehement, delicate in their instincts as a dog's or an infant's; he will detect the step of any one dear to him in a crowd, and burst into tears, if not kindly spoken to.[18]

Tom's status as an essentially freakish attraction was also reinforced by the regular presence at his concerts of white musicians and reviewers who had come for the express purpose of discrediting him as a musician of any real talent or sensibility. As one tendentious observer described a concert given by Tom during the last decade of his life, "His performance was accompanied by grunting, horrible facial contortions, and an inability to control his bladder onstage, but he perfectly duplicated, including mistakes, any selection played by a member of the audience."[19]

Even the few attempts by contemporary critics to sympathetically or even soberly assess Tom as a musician usually stroked him with one hand while slapping him with the other. For instance, the entry on Tom in *A Handbook of American Music and Musicians,* published in 1886, read:

Blind Tom cannot be classed as a musician in a strict sense of the word, having never been educated as such, and consequently his few compositions are of no value. Yet his musical talents are indisputable, and that he is in some respects a player of exceptional ability is also equally true. In fact, his seems to be one of nature's eccentrical bestowals of genius with which we sometimes meet, but difficult to be explained or accounted for.[20]

In the immediate aftermath of the Civil War, the self-consciously normalized image of black folk culture, represented by groups like the Fisk Jubilee Singers, was emerging as a challenge to the minstrel show stereotyping of blacks as buffoons and miscreants and the freak show presentation of all nonwhites as aberrant and socially unassimilable demi-humans who either came from or belonged somewhere else.

The types of music that Tom performed further highlighted his position outside of African American musical culture as such. Claims were made that Tom had perfect memory of three thousand to five thousand classical pieces, which he could play immediately upon request, and that he may have "composed" as many as one hundred more. The best known of these compositions was "The Battle of Manassas." This work owed much of its popularity to the fact that it was presented as an aural re-creation of one of the South's greatest victories. During the Civil War and afterward, its rousing chords and rhythms could be emotionally appropriated by Southern audiences in their efforts to convince themselves and their Northern sympathizers that blacks, even those as handicapped as Tom, knew that slavery had been in their best interests and were actively committed to the Southern cause and way of life.

Although a Bethune of some sort maintained control of Tom until his death, as slavery ended, one of the first and in some ways the most culturally telling attempts to wrest him away from the Bethune family was made by the black promoter Tabbs Gross, who fancied himself a black P. T. Barnum. According to Gross, in 1865 he purchased Tom for $20,000 from Colonel Bethune, who later reneged on the deal while refusing to refund Gross's "down payment." Gross's attempt to "buy" Tom from Bethune, certainly without any input from the by-then sixteen-year-old and technically free Tom himself, was not made any less exploitative by the fact that Gross was both a black man and, like Tom, a former slave. Tom's blindness alone, however, would not have enabled men like Colonel Bethune and Gross to so fully objectify him if other aspects of his life as a disabled person had not rendered him particularly vulnerable to such exploitation.

Throughout his career, it was the disturbing particularity of Tom's behavior as an "idiotic" black man, not his sightlessness, that grounded his "enfreakment" and prevented his auditors from actually "hearing" his music as music. It was also on the basis of his "feeblemindeness" that Tom could so easily be turned into a slave by another name after the legal grounding for his actual slavery had been nullified. By having Tom declared incompetent over the objections of his parents, Colonel Bethune, after the war, managed to place Tom in a condition of indenture that allowed the Bethune family to maintain absolute legal control over him and his earnings. The Bethunes maintained this "ownership" until February of 1884. After the accidental death of the colonel's son John Bethune, who had acquired control of Tom upon the colonel's death in 1883, John's estranged wife, Eliza (or Elise) Stutzbach Bethune, joined forces with Tom's mother, Charity Wiggins, in a court case against the Bethune family. The women's eventual success in this case gave Wiggins custody of her son. However, with no real means of providing for him, she turned Tom over to Stutzbach Bethune and her new husband, A. J. Lerche, who took over management of Tom's concert schedule and career.

In a gesture explicitly designed to counter the Bethune family's positioning of Tom as "a member of the family" who had been unfairly spirited away from them by the heartless forces of an impersonal and racially obtuse Northern court, the Lerches capitalized upon the publicity that the trial had received and attempted to reinvent Tom as a self-consciously active musical agent finally able to go before the public as his "real" self. Advertising him as "the last slave set free by order of the Supreme Court of the United States," they attempted to place him in the emerging post-minstrel musical culture of the early twentieth century.[21] Still, even as an ostensibly free man, Tom's appeal to black audiences was minimal, and the Lerches' refashioning of him as a "modern" man was, for the most part, a failure.[22] Although African Americans of the period recognized Tom as one of their own, this recognition rarely went beyond acknowledging him as a gifted musician and then moving on to the promotion of less complicated and disturbing figures. Despite the prominence that he had enjoyed for decades, long before his death, Tom's servitude, in whatever form it had taken, had become a nonissue for most blacks.

When considered in the specific context of post-Emancipation notions of black uplift, however, the failure of prominent African Americans to give Tom's situation any sustained attention is not surprising. P. Joy Rouse points out that black journalists in the nineteenth century "offered a representation of African Americans that countered racist stereotypes and worked to establish a citizen-specific African-American identity."[23] The legitimation of blacks as citizens that was being undertaken in the black press functioned as a challenge to the framing of racial and physical difference as monstrosity, which was being developed elsewhere in American public culture.

In their efforts to counter the newly charged and more specifically politicized racial denigration that was being directed at blacks in the postbellum period, African American journalists and public figures attempted to fashion the most conservative and circumspect social identities possible. Therefore, a connection with Tom had very little to offer to those whom Frankie Hutton describes as "a beleaguered, free people striving for vindication, uplift, and idealistically, for acceptance."[24]

Except in their most sentimentally appropriable forms, in the late nineteenth century, neither blackness nor disability had become culturally visible as a distinct but fully human way of being human. Therefore, there were few attempts by his contemporaries to positively correlate Tom's career and life with those of other blind and disabled people of the period. Still, swimming against the tide of the racist denigration to which he was usually subjected, those seeking to broaden Tom's appeal made sporadic efforts to incorporate him into the culture of sentimentality. Rosemarie Garland Thomson notes that "sentimentality was the production and demonstration of a certain affect that structured a social relationship between the person who could show fine feeling and the one who could induce it."[25] Therefore, efforts to "sentimentalize" Tom tried to reposition him as an example of one of the primary markers of nineteenth-century sentimentalism, "the gentle, grateful, afflicted child."[26] For instance, in a work supposedly authored by "Tom," the poet sighs:

> Oh, tell me the form of the soft summer air,
> That tosses so gently the curls of my hair;
> It breathes on my lips, it fans my warm cheek,
> Yet gives me no answer, though often I speak;
> I feel it play o'er me, refreshing and kind,
> Yet I cannot touch it—I'm blind, oh, I'm blind.
>
> And music, what is it, and where does it dwell?
> I sink and I rise with its cadence and swell,
> While it touches my heart with its deep thrilling strain,
> Till pleasure, till pleasure is turned into pain.
> What brightness of hue is with music combined?
> Will any one tell me?—I'm blind, oh, I'm blind.
>
> The perfume of flowers that are hovering nigh–
> And what are they—on what kind of wings do they fly?
> Are not they sweet angels, who come to delight
> A poor little boy who knows not of sight?
> The sun, moon, and stars, are to me undefined,
> Oh, tell me what light is—I'm blind, oh, I'm blind.[27]

Rather than offering his fans a window into Tom's mind, this poem more reasonably reveals the extent to which, as his celebrity grew, the reality of Tom's life in pre- and postbellum America, as a multiply impaired black man whose vocabulary may have consisted of as few as one hundred words, gave way to increasingly desperate attempts to maintain and diversify his market value. Instead of providing evidence of rational subjectivity and validating Tom's creative agency, this poem, like most of the works and documents attributed to and inspired by Tom, more specifically served the needs of those who were variously invested in using him to further their own economic and political aims. In fact, given that this is the only poem "by" Tom that is extant, to the limited extent that it was actually circulated and read, it may simply have reinforced his detractors' suspicion that Tom was little more than a ventriloquized cipher incapable of all but a form of unconscious but astounding musical expression.

One of the few intensive attempts by one of Tom's black contemporaries to recuperate or "counter-ventriloquize" him for the cause of racial uplift was the poet James D. Corrothers's poem "Blind Tom, Singing," which was published in May of 1901 in the *Southern Workman,* the official journal of the Hampton Normal and Agricultural Institute. In its rhetorical particulars, Corrothers's poem attempts to wrest Tom away from both the sentimental reconstruction of him as a functionally arrested but emotionally pure child of nature and the racist positioning of him as an exemplary instance of unassimilable black manhood:

∽ I

> Long, long ago I saw Blind Tom.
> The noisy audience became calm,
> And a hush fell o'er the whispering din,
> When the blind musician was led in.
> A moment vacantly he stood,
> 'Till, moved by some mysterious mood,
> The while the inspiration burned,
> He, to the harp that waited, turned,
> And, seated there at graceful ease,
> He swept his hands along the keys,
> Awaking sound so soft and clear
> That Silence bent with eager ear
> Its faintest whisperings to hear.
> He clapped his hands like a little child,
> And sang in accents low and mild:
> "Dem a gates ajar I'm boun' to see,
> Dem a gates ajar I'm boun' to see,
> Dem a gates ajar I'm boun to see,
> O, sinner fare you well."

∽ II

> He turned those sightless eyes to God,

His thoughts in fields of fancy trod,
Where songs unsung and notes unheard,
And sweeter sounds than song of bird,
Floating on vapory mist of light,
Descended 'round the poor blind wight,
Plashing like rain drops o'er the keys!
And sobbed in tender symphonies
O'er flowery dells where silver streams
Fell tinkling thro' a land of dreams.
He paused, and in a moment more,
We heard a cataract's loud uproar,
And rumbling thunder rolled afar,
And maddened cannon bellowed war;
The drums beat and the fifers blew
Many an old tune that we knew.
Then all was hushed, and solemnly
The curtain of eternity
Arose; and down the star-lit blue
Of the vast heavens great angels flew,
In happy band, to drift along
On the blind singer's rapturous song:
"Dah's room a 'nuff in heben, I know,
Dah's room a 'nuff in heben, I know,
Dah's room a 'nuff in heben, I know,
O, sinner, fare you well."

ᙓ III

He paused, as if some power before
Commanded him to touch no more
His throbbing, ivory plaything. And
Obedient to that command,
He ceased, and gazed in thankful mood
Toward the Giver of all good.
(O Father, if to all could come
The things revealed to poor Blind Tom,
We, too, would clap our hands in glee,
Rejoiced thy wondrous truths to see.
The scales would leave our blinded eyes,
And earth would be a paradise
Where creed and color, tongue and clime

Would melt away like morning rime;
And, like poor Tom, with self unsought,
All should make melody untaught.)
Long, long with upturned face he stood
As gazing on some heavenly flood.
And no man dared to speak a word—
No soul in that vast audience stirred.
For well we knew that where he stood,
The blind musician talked with God;
Nor did we doubt the silent prayer
Was granted as we watched him there;
For even as he turned to go,
We heard him singing, sweet and low:
"A starry crown I'm a-goin' foh to wear,
A starry crown I'm a-goin' foh to wear,
A starry crown I'm a-goin foh to wear—
O, sinner, fare you well."

The "black" dialect that is placed in Tom's mouth in "Blind Tom, Singing" serves to counter the linguistically "white" persona that characterizes the poem that had actually been attributed to him. Alternatively, Corrothers attempts to place Tom within the culture of black folk expression that was beginning, albeit in Europeanized forms, to be deployed by black Americans like the Fisk Jubilee Singers and the poets Paul Laurence Dunbar and James Weldon Johnson. These artists sought to establish the humanity of African Americans by crafting recognizably distinct and "black," but unquestionably self-aware, aesthetic forms and modes of expression. In Corrothers's poem, Tom emerges as a saintly and indicatively black figure whose innate decency and spirituality serve as a rebuke to those who sought to deny him, and by implication other blacks, possession of those qualities and thereby full membership in the family of man.

The failure by Tom's champions on both sides of the racial divide to successfully construct him as a sentimental object is telling in that, because of the specific nature of blindness as a disabling condition, all blind performers to varying degrees have displayed some of the characteristics that made the "Blind Tom" phenomenon possible. Although the evidence of the "feeble-mindedness" that Tom often displayed on stage was used to ground the most explicitly racist comments, reviews of Tom's public appearances offer little recognition of the fact that some of the more "disturbing" aspects of his onstage behavior could be attributed to his congenital blindness, and not to his mental deficits as such.

We can, for instance, conjecture that as a congenitally blind person, Tom regularly experienced what is called "the illusion of privacy."[28] This is the difficulty that blind people have in remembering all the time that they can be seen. For instance, Elizabeth C. Perry and F. Hampton Roy point out that "a high priority in instruction of the congenitally blind is the significance of good manners and personal appearance. As they have never seen anything displeasing, they are unaware of the impression made on sighted persons by observing someone chewing his food with his mouth open, the importance of color combinations in dress, the distastefulness [*sic*] to the sighted public of bizarre facial expressions, mannerisms and dress."[29] There is no evidence that the Bethune family made any instructive efforts, beyond those necessary to control him, to familiarize Tom with the etiquette of interaction that other blind people learned naturally in their growth into social awareness. In fact, the Bethunes' desire to maintain control of Tom may have actively inhibited such instruction. This failure to normalize Tom's behavior is especially significant when one considers that the illusion of privacy that Tom experienced in the countless hours that he spent on stage before generally and sometimes hostilely silent audiences may have been much greater than that of a private blind person, whose personal and conversational interactions would have more consistently acclimated him or her to the normative expectations of other people.

An especially significant aspect of the illusion of privacy that the congenitally blind are actively taught to recognize and control is the public display of those mannerisms that in blindness research have come, albeit problematically, to be called "blindisms." Although Tom's mental impairment is undeniable, his seemingly uncontrolled physical gestures, rather than being evidence of his "idiocy," may simply have been blindisms generated by his congenital sightlessness. Berthold Lowenfield notes, "Swaying the body, turning the head often quite rapidly, rocking back and forth, thrusting the fingers into the eyes or the mouth, manipulating the lips, the ears, or nose, or if the child has some sight, moving the hands before the eyes so that the change of light and shadow can be observed are some of these mannerisms."[30] Certainly, the concept of "blindisms"—one that was not available to Tom's contemporaries—makes it possible for us to understand and naturalize some of the more commented-upon aspects of Tom's "odd" onstage behavior.[31]

For instance, with the specificity of blindisms in mind as possible components of the stage presences of blind performers, we must certainly reconsider Thomas L. Riis's attempt to position Tom as a precursor to rock and roll. Riis has suggested that "one other explanation for Tom's gyrations and eccentric movements could be that they demonstrate the same sort of body language we now associate with the early history of rock-and-roll."[32] Riis states that "once one gets used to the idea of posing Little Richard or Stevie Wonder next to the filigreed fixtures of a mid-19th-century sitting room, the furor over Tom starts to make sense."[33] Riis then asks, "If teenagers of the 1950's and 1960's were driven to frenzies by James Brown and Elvis Presley, how much greater the reaction might have been from stiff-backed young people in hoop skirts or starched collars when faced with the flamboyant abandon of Blind Tom?"[34]

Elizabeth Ezra observes that "entertainment forms are expressions of community, forums in which people interact in conscious affirmation of their shared experiences."[35] Despite its entertainment value, nothing in the literature on Tom suggests that audience reactions to his performances in any way resembled the scenario that Riis constructs. The idea that in the years immediately before and after the Civil War, white and usually Southern audiences would, en masse, abandon their social investments in white supremacy upon sight of Tom's "Presleyesque gyrations" is, at best, unrealistic. Beyond that, the notion that such audiences would then publicly respond to a multiply impaired black man with expressions of emotional identification and cross-racial sexual attraction is even more unlikely. Regardless of their degree of respect for Tom's musical proficiency, Tom's exposure to throngs of gawking audiences, given the inability of his generally white listeners to even consider modeling themselves on any black person, particularly on one who looked and behaved like Tom, could only serve to heighten and validate his audiences' sense of the essential "freakishness" of both blackness and disability.[36]

Of all of Tom's gifts, however, the one that was recognized by even his most vehement critics was his possession of "absolute pitch"—"the ability to identify a musical sound without the help of a reference sound."[37] The willingness of his detractors to acknowledge this component of Tom's "genius," when all of his other talents were either contested or dismissed by some faction, perhaps stemmed from the fact that absolute or perfect pitch has generally been considered an essentially instinctive and mechanical psycho-physiological trait, rather than a musical achievement as such.

The claim made by Darold Treffert and others that Tom died "lonely and alone" is not supported by the evidence.[38] Still, in the wake of critiques like Louis Moreau Gottschalk's and the general disinterest of a growing cadre of New Negroes in someone as problematically old-guard as Tom, it is true that by the time of his death from a stroke in 1908, as indicated by the obituary published in the *New York Times* of 15 June 1908, Tom was an all but forgotten footnote in American musical history.

Although a number of blind black performers would emerge in the immediate wake of Tom's rise and fall, the most culturally important of Tom's successors by far was "Blind" William Boone (1864–1927). William Boone was born in Warrensburg, Missouri, in the Federal camp of the Seventh Militia Company, to a slave mother who had been taken as contraband and, most likely, a white soldier. At the age of six months, after his mother had relocated to Warrensburg, he underwent an operation in which both of his eyes were removed as a result of what was then called "brain fever," a condition that was most likely encephalitis or meningitis.[39] Boone and his mother thrived in Warrensburg, and the town's white citizens later arranged for the clever and well-liked nine-year-old to attend the Missouri School for the Blind in St. Louis. Although at the age of twelve Boone was expelled for spending too much time in the black tenderloin district, it was in St. Louis that he had his first exposure to the emerging culture of ragtime music, which would play a decisive role in his music and life.

Immediately after Tom's death, Blind Boone emerged as the most talented, successful, and self-consciously focused challenger to the racist worldview that had both generated Tom's career and sustained his exploitation. Central to this success was Boone's absolute resistance to the kind of "enfreakment" that had characterized almost every aspect of Tom's life and career. Boone's manager, an inexhaustibly ambitious exslave named John Lange Jr., programmatically presented Boone as a new and radically improved version of what he considered a hopelessly problematic original. Melissa Fuell, a member of the Blind Boone troop, in her authorized biography of Boone, described what happened after Tom performed at a festival in Columbia, Missouri, in 1879:

> He [Lange] thought of how he would make Willie, not only Tom's equal but endeavor to make him far the superior. He would let him hear the masters; he would take him daily to the best artists the town afforded, and let him hear them interpret the highest class of

music written; he would keep him posted on the current as well as past events, so that he would be as well read as any man with perfect eyesight. He would have his little favorite grow up to be a man among men and not in the class of idiots as was the unfortunate lot of "Blind Tom."[40]

As this passage indicates, Boone's advisors and associates made a concerted effort to prevent him from being subjected to the dehumanizing narratives that had defined both Tom's blindness and his blackness. Commentators, describing Boone, went to great pains to point out that "his playing [was] remarkable, not because of his blindness, but because of his artistic excellence." Boone's official motto, "Merit, Not Sympathy Wins," made that point explicitly clear.[41]

Boone attained mastery of the light classical pieces in vogue with the bourgeois white audiences who had flocked to see Tom, but it was syncopated ragtime pieces, and the skills that he learned in the black demimonde, that provided him with biracial options beyond Tom's musical purview and appeal. Teresa L. Reed points out that "by the late 1800s, a distinctive type of rhythmic syncopation was widely recognized as a defining characteristic of African-American music."[42] Ragtime offered Boone a means of decisively differentiating himself from Tom and positioning himself as a full-fledged member of the world of black musical modernity. Unlike Tom, whose appeal for the few blacks who could afford to attend his performances was minimal, Blind Boone, over the course of his career, became equally popular with black and white audiences. His command of both the "classics" and the "rags," the "coon" songs of the minstrel shows and black spirituals, all of which he performed with seemingly unself-conscious ease, made him a consummate all-around performer at the very moment when the demand for such artists was becoming greater than the supply.[43] Despite the range of his musical competencies, it was the rise of ragtime and the relative independence that this world made available to black performers that allowed Boone to achieve such a high level of economic success and positive recognition as both a musician and a black (but, crucially, not too black) man.

Although Lange was fully committed to presenting the biracial Boone as a "black" man, Boone's attractively hybrid appearance undoubtedly lessened the potentially threatening prospect of "social equality" that his competence and appeal to white audiences might have engendered had he, like Tom, been both more specifically "Negroid" and more obviously disabled. David A. Jasen and Trebor Jay Tichenor observe that "in an age of rigid racial divisions, ragtime appeared as a racially ambiguous commodity whose earliest composers had no common racial identity."[44] As Melissa Fuell described Boone in later life: "He is five feet five inches in height and very supple and active. His hands are short with delicately formed fingers, small feet, large head, with the same lines and shape of Beethoven's. He has a rich mulatto complexion and long black curly hair, very silken-looking and wavy."[45] In the new cultural environment, Boone's evident "blackness" gave him a distinct transracial market value that he would not have had if he had been white, and his blindness neutralized the sexual threat that an attractive, black, unimpaired man would have presented in a world always on the lookout for signs of black male presumptuousness.[46]

For the audiences of his day, a Blind Boone concert functioned as a musical articulation of the utopian possibility of physical and cultural coexistence that grounded the positions and appeal of conservative black figures like Booker T. Washington, while also appealing to blacks whose desires were neither assimilationist nor "proper."

Boone's consistent referencing of the minstrel tradition, long after it had begun to be actively criticized by more "progressive" figures in what W. E. B. DuBois called "The Talented Tenth," also served to neutralize the threat that his talent and physical attractiveness presented to notions of white supremacy.[47] Derek B. Scott observes that "the minstrel show enabled the already racially mixed white Americans to develop a sense of national identity and to perceive the place of black Americans within that identity."[48] Reflecting this need to maintain an aesthetic hierarchy in which black cultural expression could be unthreateningly presented to white audiences, "Boone would not only play the standard classics of Liszt, Chopin, and Beethoven, but he would also include raggy Negro music. After the first intermission he would say, 'Now I'll put the cookies on the lower shelf where everyone can reach them,' and he would launch into one of his Negro folk medleys."[49]

Boone's racial ambiguity may also account for the way in which traits that he and Tom might have shared as blind men were read very differently in the journalistic accounts of the period. For instance, rather than being ridiculed as a sign of his otherness, Boone's blindisms were often discounted and even romanticized. One reviewer described what he called Boone's "peculiarity": "His body is constantly in a swing motion

which reminds one of the everbowing Gaston, the polite French character of comic-sheet fame."[50] Another observed the pianist's onstage de-
meanor: "The great shaggy head of the musician swayed back and forth
in regular cadence, while the veteran's broad smile and occasional cackles
of laughter kept his audience in an uproar of merriment."[51]

Still, despite the efforts of his champions to position Boone as a modern entertainer, his life and career would regularly be amalgamated into
the racist space that the Blind Tom phenomenon had generated. One of
the most notable instances of this can be found in Willa Cather's 1918
novel *My Ántonia*. In her portrait of the figure that she calls Blind d'Arnault, Cather freely grafts Tom's plantation history and mental impairment onto a negatively racialized description of Boone's physical appearance, thereby creating a portrait that exactly accomplishes the erasure of
Boone's difference from Tom—a difference that Boone and Lange had
worked assiduously to establish. Of d'Arnault, Cather writes: "He was a
heavy, bulky mulatto, on short legs, and he came tapping the floor in
front of him with his gold-headed cane. His yellow face was lifted in the
light, with a show of white teeth, all grinning, and his shrunken paper
eyelids lay motionless over his blind eyes."[52] It is, however, in her description of the "actual" Blind d'Arnault concert that Cather most explicitly
reproduces the simultaneously appreciative and denigrating tone that
characterized so many reactions to Tom's performances. According to
Cather, "As piano playing, it was perhaps abominable, but as music it was
something real, vitalized by a sense of rhythm that was stronger than his
other physical senses,—that not only filled his dark mind, but worried his
body incessantly. To hear him, to watch him, was to see a negro [*sic*] enjoying himself as only a negro can."[53]

While trafficking freely in the slavery-derived investment in black difference that was given all but free rein in the writings of the period,
Cather's image of Blind d'Arnault also reflects the more complex notions
of race and artistry that were being generated by the emergence of the
ragtime world in which Boone would become a key player. William J.
Schafer and Johannes Riedel describe the mainstream white press's response to the emergence of ragtime as a distinct musical form: "There is a
persistent strand of what might be termed 'aesthetic Darwinism' invoked
by both pro-ragtime and anti-ragtime critics. This is the frequently expressed notion that there is something fundamentally 'primitive' or 'sav-
age' in black music, an element appealing to the bestial in the listener and
provoking him to wickedness, lewdness, or at best indecorousness."[54]

Although they were not nearly as problematic as Blind Tom and freak show performers like the Siamese twins the McKoy Sisters and William Henry Johnson (Barnum's "What Is It"), Boone and even Scott Joplin, the greatest ragtime composer, as ragtimers, were still outside the circuit of excellence that the more self-consciously upright members of the black elite considered good for the race's image.[55] These mandarins took the position that the only musical space that could fully legitimate blacks was European-style "art music." They were wary of the regressive purposes to which they felt a link between ragtime and black identity could be put. Penelope Bullock reports that the purpose of the most significant black music periodical of the time, the *Negro Music Journal,* "was to promote an interest in good music, they were not including ragtime and other popular music."[56]

In his final years, Boone's ability to attract new listeners would be hampered by his resistance to jazz, which he dismissively called "foolish talk."[57] Still, no other blind black performer of the period managed to achieve the level of personal autonomy and transracial acceptance that Lange orchestrated for his protégé and that, with declining returns, Boone maintained after Lange's death. In words that explicitly prefigure statements that his most illustrious successor, Stevie Wonder, would make many decades later, Boone often asserted that "blindness has not affected my disposition. It has never made me at outs with the world. . . . I regard my blindness as a blessing for had I not been blind I would not have given the inspiration to the world that I have."[58] Although this may have been wishful thinking, in another place and time, perhaps Blind Tom himself would have echoed these sentiments.

CHAPTER 2

Blind in Blue

Blindness and Identity in the Blues Tradition

It will quickly become apparent to anyone who casts even a cursory glance at writings on American blues music that in the first two decades of its recorded history, from approximately 1920 to 1945, the word "blind" functioned as a professional surname for a startling number of African American musicians.[1] In fact, one of the most significant aspects of the existence of blind performers in such large numbers in Southern black communities during this time is the extent to which their presence seems to have simply been taken for granted by their contemporaries.[2] After considering the lives and music of some of the best-known and most culturally significant of these artists, it becomes clear that sometimes unwittingly and at other times intentionally, these men and their admirers often minimized or deflected attention away from the more challenging and individualizing aspects of their lives as people with disabilities.[3]

If, as B. B. King has declared, "To be a blues singer is like having to be black twice," the lives and careers of blind blues singers suggest that—until the early 1960s, when they became the darlings of the folk revivalists—being a blind blues singer was often like having to be black at least three times. In one of the few essays that have attempted to account for this excess, Joseph Witek has argued that "one of the main ways blindness functions in blues discourse [is] as a sign of Otherness."[4] According to Witek, "The romanticized stereotype of the blind bluesman . . . begging on the corner with his tin cup, ennobled by his suffering, in communion with his Muse, is an image of black powerlessness that some Americans may find comforting. But the voices of the bluesmen themselves tell a different story."[5] However, what Witek and the few other writers who have specifically examined the phenomenon of the blind blues singer have generally failed to explore is the fact that, although blind bluesmen had many stories to tell, one of the stories in which they had the least interest seems to have been the story of blindness itself.[6] In the Southern communities from which they emerged, rather than being seen or seeing themselves primarily as musical artists, blind bluesmen functioned as best they could simply as men who were attempting to make a living in one of the few ways available to them. This was particularly true in social circumstances like those in the rural South of the 1920s and 1930s, where blindness was not nearly as uncommon a condition as it is today.

The rarity of songs dealing explicitly with blindness in the repertoires of blind bluesmen is especially interesting when one considers that the overwhelming majority of blues songs are sung from the first-person perspective. Teresa L. Reed writes that "blues lyrics of the 1920s, 1930s, and 1940s tend to contain highly descriptive, autobiographical material full of explanations about the nature of, and reasons for, the poet's emotional state."[7] The resistance to consistently giving blindness autobiographical or thematic centrality in their songs reflects the complex social and professional conditions that blind bluesmen faced as performers in an essentially folk form of musical expression.

It is important to remember that the tag "blind" was more often than not placed on the performer by the record company and may not have reflected the singer's personal self-identification. The fact that so few songs by blind bluesmen deal explicitly with blindness undoubtedly reflects these performers' desire to avoid the "interaction strain" and the loss of communicative intimacy that such personalized material would have engendered.[8] Given the call-and-response dynamic and the intimacy that grounded the relationship between blues performers and their audiences, specific references to an individual's blindness would have compromised the descriptive generality of his songs and, after a while, alienated or perhaps simply bored his generally sighted and unknowingly ocularcentric listeners. Herbert C. Covey argues: "Folk societies did not develop elaborate systems of measuring individuals and individual success. Thus, people with disabilities were not perceived as being dramatically different from others but rather as members of the community."[9]

Rather than offering, as they may initially seem to, a straightforward articulation of the singer's individual experience or state of mind, blues songs are in fact one of the most "other"-directed forms of musical expression. Throughout the corpus of their lyrics, blind bluesmen seem to have been particularly sensitive to the possibility that focusing on their sightlessness in their songs would have "othered" them in the sighted eyes of their audiences much more fully than the simple fact of their visual impairments. This "othering" would have served only to compromise their naturalized positions in the blues community and their effectiveness as entertainers at the frolics, dances, picnics, and other social gatherings at which they were often called upon to perform.

Even for those performers who had once been sighted, details about the causes of their visual impairment and the particulars of their lives as blind persons would have been difficult to comfortably insert into the repertoire of standard or "wandering" phrases that were constantly being reworked in early blues songs. Making a virtue of necessity in their efforts to support themselves, blind performers of the 1920s and 1930s often naturalized their condition so thoroughly that their audiences and sighted peers sometimes had difficulty believing that a particular performer was "really" blind. Certainly, many of these men negotiated their environment with a degree of self-assurance and success that for the sighted seemed incredible and, at times, even supernatural.[10] However, close examination of their lives and careers, in conjunction with the demystifying results of research by a range of observers, reveals that the success of the best known blind bluesmen, like that of blind performers across all genres of music, is not as difficult to explain as it may initially seem. For most of these performers, their successful physical passage through the spaces that they inhabited was not enabled by any blindness-generated corporeal superpowers, but primarily by specialized training, personal drive, and—at crucial moments—the availability of often professionally trained sighted and blind helpers to assist them in overcoming the various obstacles that they faced.[11] Nonetheless, far too often, sober recognition of the mechanics of the achievements of blind people in mobility and environmental awareness has been subordinated to fantastic and essentially dehumanizing tales of specialness.

Historically, the most common and, in many cases, the most pernicious of these fictions is the idea of "the vicariate of the senses," or what is now more commonly called "sensory compensation." This is the notion that blind people develop new or heightened senses to compensate for their inability to see. Patrick Trevor-Roper observes:

Until the turn of the century, there were constant references to the blind man's development of extra senses that could divine colours in cloth, project the sense of touch at arm's length, and make it possible to feel radiations that ordinary mortals never know. Indeed, the more fanciful of the blind—perhaps in whimsy, perhaps in despair—would sometimes encourage these investigations by talking of the obscure skin contractions experienced as they approached obstacles. But reason gradually prevailed and it became apparent that the blind did little more than concentrate their attention and awareness.[12]

Such notions did not die at the turn of the century, however. For instance, in a consideration of the life of the singer Blind Willie McTell, the noted blues scholar William Barlow references the idea of sensory compensation when he suggests that "his [McTell's] loss of sight did not hinder his mobility; instead it caused him to develop sonar."[13] Here, the obviously untenable idea that the inability to see could ever not be a hindrance to mobility reveals the sometimes extreme resistance of the unimpaired to fully considering or acknowledging the reality of an admired disabled person's condition. The truth is that blind people, as would be expected when one considers their inability to orient themselves by reading visual cues, are especially susceptible to geographical disorientation.

While not nearly the magic bullet that Barlow's statement suggests, a more prosaic version of the "sonar" that Barlow attributes to McTell and that a range of commentators have "recognized" in blind performers over the years is an ability that most blind people do possess to some functionally useful degree. More appropriately called "echo location" or "the obstacle sense," this skill, studies have indicated, is based primarily on hearing and the ability to register air currents. It is one that even the sighted can develop with startling speed when blindfolded or placed in conditions of total darkness. As early as 1932, Richard Slayton French could write that while "the popular mind dearly loves mystery . . . this power, which actually does exist, is not at all mysterious and yields itself readily to rational explanation. It is possessed by many persons of normal sense endowment, who experience, when advancing in total darkness, a feeling of nearness of objects."[14] In other words, those blind persons who manage to move through public spaces with such self-assurance do so not by way of sensory compensation, but through heightened and systematically trained "sensory alertness." This is "the habit of mentally registering sensory stimuli and selectively interpreting those stimuli that are necessary for the performance of desired activities without sight or with very limited vision."[15]

Another consistently misrecognized aspect of the work of blind blues singers is what can be called "lyrical passing." These are instances in which a blind performer sings from and uses descriptive imagery seemingly indicative of the perspective of a sighted person. This kind of "passing" has been considered especially noteworthy when it occurs in the work of performers like Blind Lemon Jefferson, who are known or believed to have been blind since birth. However, when placed in the performative contexts that generated the bluesmen's songs, the use of such imagery is no more unusual or worthy of special comment than is the use of what may seem to be "visual" imagery by blind people in general. As Rod Michalko points out, "It would be odd for a blind person to invoke competence and say, instead of 'see you later,' 'feel you later' or 'hear you later.'"[16]

It is the almost trivially basic fact that the primary function of linguistic interaction is to facilitate communication, not to reveal for its own sake the singularity of one's perspective, that has been consistently overlooked by those listeners who have been surprised by the "visual" images that figure so prominently in the work of blind singers and songwriters. Because the linguistic environments into which both blind people and the sighted are born are generated by interpersonal interaction, it is in fact hard to even imagine how the processes of normal life could support the development of an alternative linguistic register that could reveal the sensory particularity of the experience of blindness with any real specificity.[17] For similar reasons, it is just as difficult to imagine how blind people, especially the adventitiously blind, could develop a verbal or linguistic system that did not more or less continuously reference an economy of sight or what functional reasons they would have for wanting to do so.

As with all singers and songwriters, it was no doubt the ability of blind bluesmen to use language in ways that were not only comprehensible to sighted audiences but emotionally appropriable by them that determined their success or failure. Certainly, blind bluesmen would have been sorely handicapped as entertainers had they not been able to authoritatively reference the visual world that their sighted audiences took for granted. In fact, the inability to deploy metaphors of sight or their substitution by types of verbal expression somehow derived from the experience of blindness would have rendered these singers irredeemably odd. Therefore, not surprisingly, the occurrence of "lyrical passing" in songs by blind bluesmen is so common that examples could be picked almost at random. For instance, in Blind Blake's song "Early Morning Blues," he sings, "When you see me sleepin' baby don't you think I'm drunk / I got one eye on my pistol and the other on your trunk."[18] Similarly, in his "Got the Blues," Blind Lemon Jefferson sings of his sweetheart, "She ain't so good looking and her teeth don't shine like pearls / But that nice disposition carries a woman all through the world."[19]

The "natural" acceptance of lyrical personae reflective of the sighted world, and the investment in linguistic normality and comprehensibility that one finds in the work of blind singers and in blind people in general, may be unconscious reflections of what R. W. White calls "effectance motivation." As White suggests, this motivation is a response to the fact that "there is an endogenous, overarching human psychological motive to be effective, to have reliable effects, to be competent in exchanges with the physical and social environment."[20] It could even be argued that blind people must often be even more motivated than the sighted when attempting to reliably affect their environment, because when assessing the effectiveness of their actions, they lack what is undoubtedly the most straightforward feedback mechanism, sight and the readable appearance of things.

It is important, however, that we recognize the differing dynamics of linguistic "passing" as they relate to congenitally as opposed to adventitiously blind people. For the congenitally blind, linguistic access to the sighted world and therefore to full communicative citizenship in an ocularcentric world must to a great extent take place through the mechanism of what theorists of blindness have called "verbalism." As Dan Tuttle and Naomi Tuttle describe this phenomenon, blind people, and especially blind children, "who hear words and then use them without the experiential base for adequate understanding are engaging in 'verbalism.'"[21]

The most comprehensive attempt to examine the role that verbalism and other "visual references" play in the work of blind blues and gospel performers are Luigi Monge's essays "The Language of Blind Lemon Jefferson: The Covert Theme of Blindness" and "Blindness Blues: Visual References in the Lyrics of Blind Pre-War Blues and Gospel Musicians." Monge's work offers a singularly detailed engagement with the linguistic and imagistic particulars of the expressivity of blind bluesmen. However, despite its many virtues, Monge's work far too often reinforces J. Van Weelden's contention that in many attempts to understand the specificity of language use by blind people, "the accusation of verbalism is frequently exaggerated or unfounded."[22] Throughout these essays, Monge's extremely broad notion of what actually constitutes a "visual reference" and therefore an instance of verbalism lessens the usefulness of much of his research. For instance, in explaining his methodology, Monge argues that

> the range of such criteria should be all-inclusive; if it is limited only to explicit mentions of vision, a great number of potentially significant submerged images could be missed. Thus, I take into account not only direct descriptions of the act of seeing, viewing, and so on, but also indirect, covert, or perhaps even inadvertent implications that paint a picture or refer to some object, person, action, or event that can only be appreciated or understood fully by visualizing it.[23]

Although his decision to cast as wide a net as possible is understandable, the idea that any image can only be "appreciated or understood *fully* by visualizing it" installs a problematic circularity at the heart of Monge's analysis.

If Monge's idea that some images can only be fully understood by "visualizing" them were as true as he seems to suggest, by definition the congenitally blind would be fundamentally incapable of the type of experiential engagement with the external world that the term "visualizing" conventionally implies. Therefore, even in the context of their own expressivity, the use of such imagery by the congenitally blind could only be considered empty and "duplicitous." Close examination reveals, however, that very few of the "visual references" that Monge finds in Jefferson's work actually require any real "visualization" in order to do the communicative work that they perform as song lyrics. For instance, Monge claims that the singer's use of a "conventional expression" like "deep blue sea" is evidence of his "remarkable concern with color" and that even as semantically vague a phrase as "Don't look for me" should be taken as a "visual reference."[24] In both of these instances, Monge fails to acknowledge or perhaps recognize the essentially metaphorical or phatic use that Jefferson is making of these phrases.[25]

Monge also seems unaware of the basic presumptuousness of assuming that Jefferson or any other blind singer should have had any qualms about using such imagery. As Donald D. Kirtley writes, "The insistence that the sightless person should eschew these metaphors is tantamount to demanding that he [*sic*] extend his blindness from the purely organic realm to that of mentation, as if he were somehow not already blind enough."[26] This is perhaps the most troubling aspect of Monge's reading of these images and of his approach to the subject of blind bluesmen generally: it unwittingly fosters the kind of pathologized image of blind people and blindness that blind people and activists for the blind community have spent decades attempting to dispel. This is the ocularcentric notion that blindness, as a lived condition, can only be experienced as a state of constant frustration. For instance, Monge concludes that "[Blind Lemon] Jefferson's vigorous reactions to his impairment have all the features of an attempt to exorcize blindness through invisibility, as if he wanted to become invisible so that no one could perceive his discomfort."[27] Still, despite blind singers' generally formulaic use of visual imagery, sometimes a blind singer's visual impairment *could* add a special dimension to lyrics that would be unremarkable if sung by a sighted person. For instance, in his song "Death Cell Blues," Blind Willie McTell sings, "They got me killed for murder, and I haven't even harmed a man. . . . They got me 'cused for forging, and I can't even write my name."[28] And in "Pistol Slapper Blues," Blind Boy Fuller sings, "I can tell / my dog / any where I hear him bark; / I can tell my rider / by I feel her in the dark."[29]

Generally, however, rather than being conditions requiring the need for "exorcism" that Monge perceives in Jefferson's lyrics, blindness and other disabilities, in the rare references made to them throughout the corpus of blues texts, are generally presented as simple facts of life that were faced and dealt with as such. For both blind and sighted blues singers of the 1920s and 1930s, impaired bodies are usually straightforwardly regarded as the actually or potentially unfortunate endpoint of bad luck or exploitation, not as something shameful enough to require explanation, rationalization, or verbal camouflage.[30] Picturing blindness and other disabling conditions simply as events that revealed the limits of their personal agency and social options enabled black workers and singers to comment with varying degrees of explicitness on the exploitation and intimidation that they experienced in their daily lives.

Not surprisingly, given the tendency of blind singers to avoid the subject of their visual impairment, it was sighted singers who most often used the notion of blindness to provide a distinct image of personal misery. For instance, one version of the traditional folk song "Limber Jim" includes these lines:

> Nigger an' a white man playing seven-up
> White man played an' ace; an' nigger feared to take it up,
> White man played ace an' nigger played a nine,
> White man died, an' nigger went blind.[31]

Similarly, it is as the dystopian endpoint of racialized exploitation that the sighted Big Bill Broonzy positions blindness in "Stump Blues":

> Now you'll never get to do me like you did my buddy Shine,
> You know you worked him down on the levee until he went real
>   stone blind.[32]

After years of revisionist scholarship that has revealed the extent to which women were read out of the early narratives of blues history, I'm sure that by now many readers are asking themselves where the women are among all of these bluesmen. There were, in fact, many issues that made "blind bluesmanship" literally that. The inability of blind and other disabled women to maintain careers as blues singers at a time when an unprecedented number of their male counterparts managed to do so with some degree of success becomes especially significant when one considers the fact that there is no reason to believe that blindness, particularly congenital blindness, afflicted black men any more frequently than it did black women during the 1920s and 1930s. Also, blindness is commonly an effect of old age, and across all U.S. ethnic groups, women are generally more long-lived than men. Because blind performers were primarily a phenomenon of the so-called country or downhome blues tradition, the lack of blind female blues singers may initially seem to simply reflect the general failure of women to thrive in that scene. Tellingly, however, the blues space that women pioneered and dominated—the world of so-called classic blues—proved to be no more accommodating of a blind woman's difference.[33]

The inability of blind black women to establish a space for themselves as blues performers may reflect the negation of entertainment value generated by the sense of social and sexual "unsoundness" that the image of a blind or obviously disabled woman can evoke for the unimpaired. Despite the often depressing subject matter of their songs, the projection of an image of glamour and emotional and social self-sufficiency, as well as an air of sexual self-confidence, was the stock and trade of the "classic" female blues singers, making the idea of a blind woman plying her trade on the vaudeville stage or in a tent show almost unthinkable.[34]

The inability of even one blind woman to achieve success as a blues singer during this period suggests that the implicit association of blindness with one of the foundational components of blues discourse, illicit sex, may have fundamentally limited the expressive parameters of blind female performers. Catherine Kudlick points out that "though most blindness is not inherited, suggestions of a blind woman's sexuality might . . . have evoked the possibility of tainting the human race."[35] Given the ideas about acceptably circumspect female behavior that are still prevalent, the image of a blind woman standing on a stage strutting her stuff or standing on a street corner singing for coins was unacceptable in a culture whose most widely disseminated image of a blind woman was that of the internationally celebrated Helen Keller as "saintly blind virgin."[36]

To some extent, this absence of blind women from the blues tradition and generally from the world of mainstream entertainment indicates the disproportionate degree to which women are affected by the "don't stare" rule that makes any type of physical difference off-limits in most public contexts. The inability of the "able-bodied" to either positively engage or ignore a disabled woman's "difference" no doubt reflects society's far greater and more normatively proscriptive investment in beauty as a marker of female physiological soundness and romantic appeal. As Sandhya Limaye among others has argued, more often than not "women with disabilities are assumed to be asexual not only socially but also biologically and psychologically."[37]

Just as they are assumed to be asexual, disabled women are also generally considered to be much more vulnerable to harm than either men or unimpaired women.[38] There could be little doubt that a blind woman, even more than a sighted one, anywhere but safely at home being watched over by her loved ones was likely to be told that she was, as the cliché goes, "asking for trouble." Even as self-sufficient a woman as the legendary Memphis Minnie could sing in "Nothing in Rambling," "I walked through the alley / With my hand in my coat / The po-lice start to shoot me / Thought it was something I stole."[39] Certainly, if the simple prospect of walking through an alley was enough to give Memphis Minnie pause, a blind woman's special vulnerability, in the various contexts of blues performance, might have been more than enough to disturb the necessary mindlessness with which a passerby might toss a dime into a blind singer's cup or laugh at a tent singer's double entendres.

Cultural awareness of the particular vulnerability of both black and disabled women as they attempted to negotiate the various social landscapes of 1920s and 1930s America is reflected in songs like Lottie Kimbrough's "Going Away Blues":

> I'm lame and blind
> Can't hardly see
> My doggone daddy turned his
> Back on me
> 'Cause I'm lame
> I can't hardly see
> I ain't got nobody to
> Really comfort me[40]

Similarly, in "Oh Oh Blues," Bert Mays sings, "Then this poor / woman's blind / and they leads her round every day / I know it's one left here to see / 'bout her / please don't use her any old way."[41]

Of course, in the lynching-crazed 1920s and 1930s, the world outside of their homes was in many ways an unprecedentedly dangerous place for all African Americans. Accordingly, the gendered demographics of labor and black men's greater presence in the more visible and volatile sectors of the public sphere may also account to a significant degree for the discrepancy between the numbers of blind male and blind female blues performers. Black male bodies that bore the marks of their passage through spaces like prisons, labor camps, and factories were much more likely than women's bodies to still be considered intact, sexually viable, and potentially entertaining. Ultimately, all of these factors combined to prevent blind women of all ethnicities from achieving public acceptance as entertainers and to create a situation in which families were much less likely to facilitate or even consider music as a money-making option for a blind girl. For instance, as late as 1973, Berthold Lowenfeld, a leading scholar on blindness, could write, "While it does not seem realistic to expect blind girls to earn a living, young blind men should early be placed in a situation where they learn to work for their bread and get used to assuming responsibility for their work."[42]

There was, however, one factor that may have trumped all of the others in stymieing blind women who might have been inclined to try their

luck singing the blues. This was the fact that these women could not expect to find a ready supply of domestically deracinated "lead girls" who
could offer services comparable to those offered to blind men by the
young boys generated in such large numbers by both the limited work options available to them in the Jim Crow South and adolescent wander-
lust. Moshe Barasch, in his examination of the representation of blind
people in Western art, observes that "one of the oldest motifs of depict-
ing, and visually identifying, the blind is . . . the almost timeless composition of the blind old man led by a young boy."[43] Extending this tradition,
blind singers and their "lead boys" were a familiar sight in the pre-De-
pression South.

In fact, the tradition of the lead boy functioned as a mode of appren-
ticeship for a number of blues singers who would go on to achieve
significant degrees of popular success and recognition. Although accounts vary as to the extent to which any particular blind performer re-
lied on lead boys, the manner in which the lead boy tradition could provide a form of mentorship for aspiring bluesmen is especially apparent in
the relationship between Blind Lemon Jefferson and Aaron Thibeaux
"T-Bone" Walker (1910–75). After serving as Jefferson's lead boy in Dallas, Walker later achieved great success with a modernized electric guitar
style greatly influenced by Jefferson's playing. Similarly, the celebrated
folk singer Josh White, who estimated that over an eleven-year period he
may have served as "lead boy" for more than thirty different blind singers,
often acknowledged the formative role that these experiences played in
his development as a musician and singer.[44]

Although they have not received the general recognition that has
been accorded blind black bluesmen, a handful of notable white blind
performers also functioned during this period. It is in fact among white
performers that we find the most musically significant relationship between a blind singer and his lead boy.[45] The evolution of Richard (Dick)
Burnett's relationship with the fiddler Leonard Rutherford into a musical partnership that lasted for over thirty-five years offers a particularly
striking example of how the "lead boy" phenomenon could function as a
type of musical and professional mentoring.[46] Recording over fifty
songs between 1926 and 1930, Burnett, like Blind Lemon Jefferson, provided the exemplary image of a blind folk performer for white Southern
audiences.[47]

Despite Burnett's appeal, the most influential and culturally significant of all white blind performers of the period was the singer and yo-

deler Riley Puckett (1894–1946), whom Allen Lowe calls "the first modern country singer."[48] As Puckett freely acknowledged, his performing style was greatly influenced by black Southern culture, and there is evidence that before his racial identity became common knowledge, his records were quite popular with black record buyers. In fact, it is the "blackness" of Puckett's sound that may have contributed to his absence from the consciousness of the average contemporary fan of country music. In any case, Lowe is probably on the right track when he suggests that if Puckett "hadn't been overweight and blind, eyes out of alignment and undisguised by dark glasses, a picture of physical awkwardness and ungainly bulk, his name might carry more of the substance of legend for contemporary country audiences, as Jimmie Rodgers' does."[49]

If Riley Puckett's access to mainstream acceptance was limited by his physical appearance and sonic hybridity, both good looks and a notably "black"-influenced sound would play a major role in the career of the most commercially successful of all white blind American musicians, the country-and-western performer Ronnie Milsap. Born blind in 1945, Milsap had over forty number-one hits on the *Billboard* country music charts, as well as a score of major crossover pop hits. Ultimately, he achieved a level of commercial success and mainstream recognition matched among American blind performers only by the superstars Ray Charles and Stevie Wonder. Tellingly, Milsap's experience of blindness as a social condition seems to have been radically different from that of the African American blind performers who both preceded and followed him. Reflecting the degree to which blindness was a much more stigmatized condition among whites in the 1940s than among blacks, Milsap wrote: "I have heard psychologists claim that ninety percent of a child's personality is formed by the age of seven. If that is true, my psychological scars are deep. I was taught to feel guilt and inferiority because I was blind. . . . My mother actually made me feel, in my young mind, that I was responsible for my own blindness."[50]

Although Milsap makes it clear that his mother's aversive reaction to his blindness was pathologically extreme and recognized as such by many members of his family and community, throughout his biography it is apparent that his Christian fundamentalist rural North Carolina family and friends considered his condition much more shameful and distressing than did the families and communities of blind black performers. The distress that Milsap's condition engendered for his loved ones was certainly exacerbated by the fact that during the first three decades of the twentieth century, blindness became a major issue of public concern and official denigration.[51] The foundation for stigmatizing blind people, reflected in Milsap's experience, had been laid by the prominence that blindness was given as a marker of physiological inferiority in the eugenic discourses that achieved their greatest degree of cultural acceptance during this period. Edwin Black asks, "Why did blindness prevention rise to the top of the eugenic agenda in the 1920s?" His answer is telling:

> Eugenicists . . . carefully added a key adjective to their cause: *hereditary*. Therefore, their drive was not to reduce blindness arising from accident or illness, but to prevent the far less common problem of "hereditary blindness." How? By banning marriage for individuals who were blind, or anyone with even a single case of blindness in his or her family. According to the plan, such individuals could also be forcibly sterilized and segregated—even if they were already married.[52]

As Black's detailed research makes clear, this scapegoating rhetoric very quickly gave "scientific" legitimacy to an image of blind people as not only corporeally unfit, but contaminatingly so.

This politicized denigration of blindness and blind people drew upon what Michael E. Monbeck calls the now "anachronistic . . . association of blindness with venereal disease."[53] Until well into the twentieth century, much blindness across ethnic groups was caused by *ophthalmia neonatorum*, "an easily preventable infection that mothers suffering from venereal disease passed to their infants and that was the major cause of blindness in the newborn."[54] As late as 1941, as much as 15 percent of all blindness in the United States was attributed to syphilis.[55] For many white Americans, the stigma that these percentages invoked was symbolized by the health status of large numbers of black Americans. Because professional health care was almost completely unavailable to African Americans in the South and their living conditions were usually cramped, a single case of syphilis or gonorrhea could quickly lead to the infection of an entire family and thereby to an epidemic of congenital syphilis and high levels of both blindness and early mortality. As a result, in the eyes of their neighbors, the white blind, especially those who were also poor, were fundamentally "blackened" by their condition.[56]

In tragically ironic ways, the very extent of venereal infection, especially among children, served to protect individual blacks from the shame that Milsap and other blind white Southerners experienced, making the visible presence of blind people in black communities less troubling for their families and friends. Edward H. Beardsley observes: "Unlike whites, few blacks associated syphilis and gonorrhea with immorality or any loss of social standing (though they did recognize VD as a health problem). Most simply concluded that they had 'bad blood,' which they felt was as treatable as bad teeth."[57]

Throughout the South, one of the enterprises that was sustained by the lack of health care options available to blacks and other poor Americans during this period was the "medicine show," which regularly used blues and country singers to attract primarily rural and working-class audiences.[58] As a prelude to selling their potions, medicine show "doctors" often used blues singers to lure those whose physical woes may not have been particularly urgent and who were drawn to the shows primarily for entertainment. Although medicine show veteran Pink Anderson claimed that "few shows wanted blind performers because of their special problems," a substantial number of blind performers, including Blind Willie McTell, Blind Blake, Simmie Dooley, and Sonny Terry, managed to find work in them.[59]

In some cases, blacks who could afford and had access to licensed medical practitioners actually preferred medicine shows because of the often cursory and disrespectful treatment that they received from "real" doctors.[60] The physician's report produced after an examination of Blind Boy Fuller for the Durham Social Security Board in 1937 reveals the simultaneously clinical and cavalier attitude with which blacks were often treated by the few white doctors who accepted them as patients:

Diagnosis: Eye condition primarily responsible for blindness.
Right eye: phthisis bulbi
Left eye: papilloma of the cornea evidently following old
             perforating ulcer

Etiological factor responsible for primary eye condition: Probably
             gonorrhea conjunctivitis

Describe the appearance of eyes, including fundi.
Right eye: fundi, phthisis bulbi, secondary glaucoma.
Left eye: as above

Central Visual Acuity:	Without glasses.	With glasses.
Right eye:	Nil	Nil
Left eye:	Nil	Nil

Prognosis (Is there any likelihood that vision could be restored by operation or treatment?)   Nil
Recommendations.   Nil
Remarks. (When should applicant be reexamined?) None.[61]

As this physician's curtness and blithe relegation of Fuller's body to the medical netherworld indicate, although Southern blacks may not have been offered any consistent health care, there was official awareness of the fact that, in order to maintain the myth of separate but equal social spheres that grounded Jim Crow society, at least token efforts had to be made to attend to ailing black bodies. Additionally, the paper trail left by these doctors reveals the recognition among white physicians and administrators that paying clinical attention to the etiological and prognostic particulars of black health problems could lead to knowledge that could be used in the war against disease and disability in the so-called general population—that is, among whites.

Because of unequal access to medical treatment and information, the numbers of blind Americans varied greatly across ethnicities and economic classes. Within these groups, however, musically talented blind people may have been more likely than the sighted to make at least token efforts to move beyond simple amateurism and attempt to support themselves or supplement their earnings by working as musicians. This tendency reflected their inability or perceived inability to perform the comparatively well-paying jobs that would draw sighted musicians away from a full-time commitment to music-making. Additionally, their impairment gave blind people, for better or worse, an option that the sighted could not consistently exercise with even remotely comparable degrees of success: begging.[62] It is possible, in fact, that even more than the white blind, blacks in this period were especially well situated both socially and psychologically to committing themselves to street singing as a "job" and to acceptance of the image of penuriousness that inevitably accompanied it.[63] Robert Scott points out that "blind beggars probably come from marginal segments of the society where commitment to the mainstream of American values is not deep; in fact, such values may be scorned. They are consequently not as vulnerable to guilt or remorse for their deliberate manipulation and exploitation of the emotions of others."[64]

Blind Lemon Jefferson, 1894–1929.
Courtesy of John Tefteller and Blues Images.

Beyond the pleasure of making music and achieving the level of self-sufficiency that it offered, street singing as a form of begging may have held a special and even subversive appeal for blind African Americans. What Bronislaw Geremek suggests of the medieval church's attitude toward beggars resonates strongly with the Jim Crow South: "Begging was seen to be humiliating not only for the beggar but also for the social group to which he belonged, to everyone linked to him by 'solidarity of status.'"[65] Because of the willingness of Jim Crow society to let blacks publicly perform acts that seemed to reinforce notions of their inferiority and lack of social worthiness, begging was a much more accepted and even professionalized activity for members of the black underclass than it was for whites. The status of street-singing blind bluesmen as "proper paupers"[66] is revealed by a letter that has survived from Blind Boy Fuller's (Fulton Allen) social worker:

> April 8, 1933
> In re: Fulton Allen (Col.)
>
> Mr. G. W. Proctor
> Chief of Police
> Durham, N.C.
>
> Dear Mr. Proctor:
>   If it meets with your approval we are glad to recommend that the above named man be allowed to make music on the streets of Durham at a place designated by you.
>   Assuring you that we are always glad to cooperate with you, I am
>
> Yours very truly
>
> W. E. Stanley
> Supt. Public Welfare[67]

For those charged with regulating the marketplace, it was not deemed necessary to recognize Allen specifically as a disabled citizen. Instead, the official position seems to have been that Fuller, who did not become completely blind until he was in his twenties, was simply a representative (black) man in need of money who, for reasons so obvious as to not need stating, should be given official access to those who had it.

The social visibility that this recognition made possible could, however, be a mixed blessing for blind street performers. As Joseph Witek observes, "A blind street singer's pay is always an ambiguous mixture of performer's fee and off-hand charity."[68] Given this ambiguity, one of the problems that singers like Fuller faced is that, despite their lack of access to most of the jobs available to sighted black men, they were regularly dropped from the welfare and blind assistance rolls when their usually meager earnings from street singing or recording were discovered.

Therefore, despite the importance of the street corner as the primary site of cultural visibility for blind bluesmen, it was the recording studio that would ultimately secure them their prominent place in African American musical history.

Some have argued that the success of blind African American musicians and their seemingly disproportionate level of prominence and promotion by white male executives during the early days of the recording industry reflect the fact that the symbolically "castrated" blind black man could be positioned as less than fully male in relation to able-bodied white masculinity.[69] In fact, since Oedipus by way of Freud, the symbolic relation between blindness and castration has become a pop-cultural commonplace. I believe, however, that rather than revealing white men's psychosexual investment in the supposed asexuality and unmanliness of blind men, the ready access to the recording studio that blind musicians were given during this period may simply reflect the greater ease with which they could be both recorded and economically exploited. The promotion of these blind men as recording artists by a range of record companies occurred at exactly the moment when black performers in general were becoming more sophisticated about the ways of the recording and publishing industries. Also, the slow but steady amelioration of the more blatant forms of racism was giving them greater opportunities for airing their grievances and for exploring a wider range of professional and personal options.

Although both Papa Charlie Jackson and the street performer Daddy Stovepipe preceded him into the recording studio, the performer whose life and career essentially inaugurated the recording histories of both country blues and blind bluesmanship is Blind Lemon Jefferson.[70] Despite the earlier success of Blind Tom and Blind Boone, Jefferson can be considered the foundational figure in the recognition of blind musical performers as significant players in the narrative of African American popular music.[71] While, in relation to his successors, not as instrumentally virtuosic as Blind Blake, as personally colorful as Blind Boy Fuller, or as widely recorded as Blind Willie McTell, Jefferson ranks as perhaps the most influential male blues performer of all time.[72] He occupies a position analogous to that of the first recorded female blues singer, Mamie Smith, in that it was the success of his debut recordings in 1926 that created the demand for the country blues that essentially signaled the end of the commercial dominance of the female "classic" blues singers.

Jefferson was born, most likely completely blind, in 1893 on a farm in

Blind Arthur Blake, 1893–1933.
Courtesy of John Tefteller and Blues Images.

Couchman, Texas. Not surprisingly, a myth that has dogged practically all blind musicians and singers at some point in their lives was a regular component of the response to Jefferson by his peers and critical readers. This was the refusal by many of these auditors, when faced with Jefferson's self-sufficiency and apparent "normality," to accept the fact that he actually was blind. However, even if it were true, as a few accounts suggest, that Jefferson may have had some residual light perception, the evidence overwhelmingly indicates that he was lacking in any functionally useful degree of vision.[73] The strongest evidence that Jefferson's blindness was both congenital and complete is the fact that there is no convincing counterevidence that it wasn't. Blindness is not simply an event or condition in the history of an individual. It is also an event in the history of his or her family and of the community of which he or she is a part. The lack of specific explanatory accounts suggesting that either disease or some kind of misadventure caused Jefferson's impairment suggests that it is unlikely that he was born sighted and later became blind. Were this the case, such a blinding event or process would inevitably have become a more stable part of the narrative of Jefferson's life, as he achieved prominence just as the causes of the sightlessness of most adventitiously blind performers became relatively easy to pinpoint. Invariably, the stories that suggest that Jefferson had once been sighted or was not completely blind tend to be the type of spectacularizing recollections that one often finds in anecdotal accounts of personal experiences with illustrious disabled people when they are being reconstructed for posterity.

Although the generally high quality of the 110 recordings that Jefferson made between the years 1926 and 1929 has rightfully been most closely considered in blues scholarship, it was ultimately Jefferson's preeminence and fierce independence, rather than any radical musical distinctiveness from other folk blues artists of his era, that established him as the incidental model for subsequent blind bluesmen as they emerged into public culture. Robert Santelli describes Jefferson as follows: "His vocal style included many of the mannerisms that would later define blues singing including an elastic, thin veneered whine. But it was Jefferson's guitar style that had the biggest impact on his contemporaries and future generations of bluesmen."[74] Jefferson's influence becomes even more remarkable when one considers the fact that both his life and his recording career were so short.

Of the various accounts of Jefferson's demise that have found their way into blues scholarship, the two most often repeated stories suggest either that he was abandoned by his driver during an intense Chicago snowstorm or that he died of a heart attack while trying to find his way home. Whatever the particulars of his death, Paramount Records responded to the loss of its biggest seller by quickly releasing a number of memorial recordings. The fact that the company saw commercial potential in memorializing Jefferson as an exemplary image of black identity and manhood reveals the degree to which, despite his disability or perhaps even because of it, his music had been received within the African American community as a particularly resonant sounding of its desires and concerns. The most notable of these memorial recordings were a song called "Wasn't It Sad about Lemon" and Reverend Emmett Dickinson's sermon "The Death of Blind Lemon Jefferson." In the latter recording, Dickinson eulogized:

> When I was informed of Lemon's death, I thought of our Lord Jesus Christ as He walked down the Jericho Road and saw a man who was born blind. And His Disciples said, "Master, who did sin? Did this Man sin or his parents, that he is a man born blind?" And Jesus Christ answered, "Neither did this man sin nor his parents sin but that I may be manifested in him." Lemon Jefferson was born blind and was cut off from the good things of this life that you and I might enjoy; he truly had a cross to bear. How many of us today are crying about the crosses we are to bear; "oh lord, this is too hard for me oh lord, my life is miserable to lead." Blind Lemon is dead. As Lemon died with the lord so did he live.[75]

Alan Govenar writes of this recording, "The sermon does little to explain the reality of Jefferson's life and death, but it is a testimony to the magnitude of his career and its importance in African-American culture."[76] The resonance of Jefferson's example is made especially clear in the continuities and differences apparent between it and the lives and careers of the blind blues singers who emerged in his wake.

The most immediately recognized and acclaimed of Jefferson's successors was Blind Blake, born in Jacksonville, Florida.[77] Over the course of the more than eighty songs that he recorded and the myriad of tracks on which he performed, Blake displayed a level of purely technical virtuosity that would only be rivaled among blind African American blues performers by his fellow guitarist Reverend Gary Davis. One critic notes of Blake that "his finger-picking guitar style represents ragtime guitar at its highest degree of perfection. His syncopated bass lines, his sudden rhythmic shifts and his smooth phrasing sometimes put him on a par with the jazz guitarists of his day."[78] Unlike Jefferson, Blake had a degree of technical prowess that made it possible for him to circulate comfortably in the burgeoning worlds of jazz and cabaret culture and that may

Blind Boy Fuller, between 1903 and 1908–41.
Courtesy of John Tefteller and Blues Images.

explain the surprisingly respectful promotional attention that he was given long before other blind bluesmen were accorded mainstream recognition as anything other than inspired primitives. For instance, in its promotional book *The Paramount Book of the Blues,* Paramount eschewed the minstrel-derived discourse that it often resorted to when describing the recordings of black performers:

> Born . . . in sunny Florida, he seems to have absorbed some of the
> sunny Florida atmosphere—disregarding the fact that nature had
> cruelly denied him a vision of other things. He could not see the
> things that others saw—but he had a better gift. A gift of inner vi-
> sion that allowed him to see things more beautiful. The pictures
> that he alone could see made him long to express them in some
> way—so he turned to music.[79]

Nonetheless, despite the high regard in which he was held by the more
discerning members of the musical world, it was not Blake who most directly succeeded Blind Lemon Jefferson as the exemplary figure of blind
bluesmanship as such. This honor went to the man known as Blind
Willie McTell.

While never as commercially successful as Blind Lemon Jefferson or
as technically gifted as Blind Blake, McTell has received more sustained
and varied recognition than perhaps any other blind blues performer.
Much of this attention can be traced to the fact that McTell's career was
exceptionally long for a blind blues performer of his generation, and his
passage through the various strata of American life was unusually wide-
ranging, as were the influences reflected in his music.[80] Although there
were long periods in which he was not recording (under any of his pseudonyms) or receiving much attention from either blues audiences or the
recording establishment, McTell seems to have never lost a sense of himself as a professional musician. Further, having attended schools for blind
people in Michigan, New York, and Georgia, McTell was especially
knowledgeable about how to access points within the network of social
services for blind people and thereby sustain himself during the fallow
periods of his life and career. When necessary, he availed himself of the
services offered by such groups as Lighthouse for the Blind, turning to
this organization for support during the last impoverished years of his
life. The training that McTell received in these institutions, especially his
ability to read Braille, may help to explain his relatively careerist approach to both music-making and life as a blind person.

During the blues revival of the 1960s, the appeal of country blues
artists like McTell who were "discovered" by young white audiences was
often heightened or perhaps even generated by the corporeal markers of
the physical wear and tear that their bodies had experienced. In one of
the most controversial passages in blues criticism, Charles Keil describes
what he called this "moldy-fig mentality":

Blind Willie McTell, 1898–1959.
Courtesy of John Tefteller and Blues Images.

The criteria for a real blues singer, implicit or explicit, are the following. Old age: the performer should preferably be more than sixty years old, blind, arthritic, and toothless. . . . Obscurity: the blues singer should not have performed in public or have made a recording in at least twenty years. . . . Correct tutelage: the singer should have played with or been taught by some legendary figure.

Sonny Terry, 1911–86.
Courtesy Cleveland State University Library.

Agrarian milieu: a bluesman should have lived the bulk of his life as
a sharecropper, coaxing mules and picking cotton, uncontaminated
by city influence.[81]

Such characterizations of the racial politics of the folk/blues revival have,
of course, been challenged. Still, it cannot be denied that a number of performers whose success with black audiences had been limited even during
their prime were given surprising new leases on life by young white men

and women who came to their performances with very different expectations and cultural frameworks than had their initial listeners.[82]

From this perspective, the most significant of these "discoveries" was undoubtedly "Sleepy" John Estes (1904–77). Although Estes had been sightless in one eye since an accident in his youth, he experienced his greatest commercial success and recognition after he became completely blind in old age and was enthusiastically embraced by folk and blues revivalists. According to Bob Groom, Estes's return to recording and performing in 1962 "astounded an almost incredulous blues world."[83] Much of Estes's appeal for these audiences stemmed from the fact that in the 1930s, when blues style began to change and become more instrumentally dynamic and "modern," Estes was "one of the few singers to maintain the less sophisticated style of accompaniment."[84] After his reemergence, regardless of the quality of the music that he produced on a given occasion, it was this sense of arrested musical development, of his sound as a literal blast from the past, that made him so striking. In conjunction with the symbolic force of his blindness, Estes's music provided an unsurpassable image and sounding of folk authenticity for young people who in many cases might never before have even heard the voice of a blind person.[85]

Like Estes, the harmonica player Sonny Terry, during the last decades of his life, also benefited from and, in many ways, actively exploited the emergence of a musical culture hungry for what fewer and fewer black performers had to offer. Although legally blind by any criteria, Terry seems to have possessed a relatively high degree of functionally useful vision. In fact, the very rarity of blind bluesmen in the folk revival scene that wrested poor black men from obscurity and fashioned them into icons of cultural authenticity may have given his condition a market value that he was loathe to reduce by revealing just how much he could see.[86] Certainly, in his stage patter and on record, Terry referenced his inability to see with more variety, consistency, and self-deprecating humor than any other blind blues performer.[87]

One of the most important and fascinating recent works relating to African American musicians and blindness is the Oscar-nominated documentary film *Genghis Blues* (1999), directed by Roko Belik. It is also a fitting document through which to close this examination of the lives and works of blind African American blues artists. The film documents the African American blues and rock singer and songwriter Paul Pena's

"Sleepy" John Estes, 1899–1977.
Courtesy of John Tefteller and Blues Images.

mastery of the Tuvan tradition of throat singing, which reflects both the drive that talented and ambitious blind performers have displayed over the years and the challenges that they have faced in their efforts to negotiate the normalizing and ableist landscapes of popular music and American life. It is both sad and telling that Pena's essentially playful mastery of this tradition would bring him the kind of attention that his profound mastery of the blues and folk-rock traditions did not.

This film, with both artistry and sensitivity, reveals the complex intersections of physical and cultural possibility as they are enacted in the lives of the physically impaired. One of the counternarratives that this film provides is the representation of the even more deracinated life that Pena is forced to live in a world in which there is no readable place for a musician with his particular set of challenges and skills.

After coming across a recording of Tuvan throat singing on a short-wave broadcast emanating from Moscow, the enthralled Pena devoted nine years to mastering the form. This effort functioned as Pena's way of reinventing himself as a musical artist after it became clear that the ability or willingness of those in his home country to recognize his talent and accommodate his condition would continue to be extremely limited. Until his death in 2005, Pena's battles with physical illness and depression and his sharp statements about the harsh realities of life for those who are both blind and poor contrasted sharply with both the relative silence about their condition that has characterized the public postures of the most successful blind performers and the romanticizing of blindness that one often finds in the writings of their sighted admirers.

Few documents have provided as stark an image of the challenges that blind people often face as does *Genghis Blues*. This disparity is especially telling when one remembers that Pena's career had such a promising start. He performed with such celebrated blues artists as T. Bone Walker, B. B. King, and Bonnie Raitt and saw his composition "Jet Airliner" become a major hit for the Steve Miller Band. However, as the corporate structure of the music industry became more firmly entrenched and its resistance to difference more pronounced, Pena found himself marginalized and eventually completely disregarded.

While the folk blues of performers like Estes and Terry survived for a while by appealing to white college audiences, it was the ostentatiously "full-bodied" blues of new singers like Muddy Waters, Howlin' Wolf, and John Lee Hooker that captured the imagination of black audiences in the 1950s and beyond. The coming of urban electrified blues in the mid-1940s signaled the beginning of the end for blind blues performers. When the dynamics of African American culture changed, and self-consciously modern musicians and singers who were straightforwardly committed to providing "up-to-date" entertainment appeared, the black audiences for blind bluesmen quickly turned away. Ironically, in whichever direction they looked, it seemed that some new type of blind performer was waiting for them. It is to these blind men (and finally women) that we now turn.

⟨☙⟩

CHAPTER 3

The Souls of Blind Folk

Blindness and Blind People in African American
Spiritual and Gospel Music

The presence of blind people as both singing subjects and observed objects in the world of African American religious music has been both obvious and uneasy: obvious because to whom could we expect them to turn but the Lord and uneasy because unease is usually the response of the unimpaired to the emergence of the impaired into public view as anything other than seekers of charity. In fact, in historical terms it is only quite recently that blind people have been accorded social recognition as something other than "ineducable mendicants, who only came to the fore when their sightless eyes were replaced by an inner vision."[1] The fact that so many blind singers have managed to achieve some success as performers of spiritual, inspirational, or gospel music may be largely attributable to the fact that for most people, spirituality and blindness have always seemed fundamentally related.[2] This is not surprising, as throughout history blind people have often been seen as both the living images of what the sighted consider to be a singularly frightening possibility and the bearers of special insight. Reflecting their awareness of the special emotional and symbolic force that blindness has for the sighted, blind spiritual and gospel singers, over the years, have had to position themselves very complexly in relation to both the possibilities of the musical forms in which they work and the expectations and anxieties of their audiences. It is black spiritual and gospel music's distinctiveness as a cultural form that seeks to both entertain and enlighten that has necessitated the particular adjustments that blind people have made in their efforts to sing the Lord's praises.

Although they evolved in tandem, in their expressive particulars, the blues and the traditions of spiritual and gospel music are very different musical and social formations. However, from the start, as performers like Blind Willie Johnson and even Blind Lemon Jefferson make clear, blind people were situated firmly at the intersection of these forms. Because they were grounded in Christian scripture, spirituals lacked the expressive autonomy that enabled the blues to function as a specifically black counternarrative to the denigrating race rhetoric of mainstream American culture. Still, like other African Americans, blind people in their songs and performances could wrench Christian scripture and hymnody from their usual contexts and make them serve the singer's more specialized purposes. From the perspective of the sighted, blind people may seem especially appropriate for singing the blues, given the apparent obviousness of what they have to be blue about. However, in spiritual contexts, the ideal blind person is usually considered to be someone who *has* the right to sing the blues, but whose faith prevents her or him from doing so.

In their fashioning of spirituals as expressive instruments, the possibility of the miraculous transcendence of an unfair but seemingly naturalized physical condition had an undeniable appeal for the slaves who crafted them from resources within their own African-derived cultures and the usable elements of Christian hymnody and theology. For instance, in Isaiah 35: 4–6 one finds heartening lines:

> Say to them that are of a fearful heart. Be strong, fear not: behold, your God will come with vengeance, even God with a recompense; he will come and save you. Then the eyes of the blind shall be opened, and the ears of the deaf shall be unstopped. Then shall the lame man leap as a hart, and the tongue of the dumb shall sing.

Through the redaction of such passages into song, the lack in most spirituals of a narrative of social agency that could bridge the space between a negative present and a more ideal future indicates that, at their inception, the spirituals were not overtly engaged in the process of crafting agendas for social change. The appropriating of these songs for the project of civil rights activism almost a century later would reveal their militant potential. This may explain why, soon after the Civil War, Europeanized versions of black spirituals by the Fisk Jubilee Singers and other groups could function as the entering wedge for the emergence of a post-minstrel black musical culture.

Although few spirituals or gospel songs reference blindness with any extended explicitness, miraculous interventions like "making the blind man see" and "making the cripple walk" can be regularly found in the corpus of these works. For instance, in the spiritual "Children, We All Shall Be Free," the singer reports that upon his return Jesus will

> Give ease to the sick, give sight to the blind,
> Enable the cripple to walk;
> He'll raise the dead from under the earth,
> And give them permission to talk.[3]

It is interesting that in these passages, comparatively mundane events such as easing the sick, curing the blind, and putting the crippled back on their feet are placed on the same conceptual plane as such fantastic and apocalyptic possibilities as raising the dead. The ease with which blindness could be brought into the matrix of sin and redemption that grounds Christian thought made disability and especially blindness too obvious a symbolic reference point for hymnists to fail to take advantage of them. For instance, few of the millions who regularly sing the lines

> Amazing grace, How sweet the sound,
> That saved a wretch like me,
> I once was lost, but now I'm found,
> *Was blind,* but now I see (emphasis added)

reflect upon the casual referencing of blindness as a state of sin in this, perhaps the best-known of all Christian hymns.

Moshe Barasch points out, "In the writings of the Fathers of the Early Church, both Greek and Latin, the state of a person (whether Jewish or gentile) before his or her conversion is described as a condition of blindness and darkness; the state after the conversion is one of seeing and light."[4] It is this association of seeing or being in the light with the transcendence of both sin and corporeality that grounds the metaphorical deployment of such terms across a range of Judeo-Christian discourses and that was deployed in early black spirituals. Throughout these songs, the disabled are positioned in relation to slavery as the slave was positioned in relation to the free. In other words, they are generally abject figures whose condition(s) represent the standard in relation to which lesser and therefore more bearable trials and tribulations could be assessed.[5]

In most spirituals that reference blindness, visual impairment is usually presented as a condition whose miraculous cure could serve as evidence of the subject's spirituality and righteousness, but whose continuing presence might indicate hidden sin and a correspondingly deserved state of dis-ease. For instance, a well-known song features the lines,

> The blind man stood on the road and cried,
> Oh, the blind man stood on the road and cried,
> Crying, oh my Lord save-a me.
> The blind man stood on the road and cried.

> Cryin': "Help me, O Lawd, if you please."
> Cryin': "O Lawd, show me de way."
> The blind man stood on de road and cried.

> When I was a sinner I stood on de way an' cried,
> Cryin': "O Lawd, show me de way."
> The blind man stood on de road and cried.[6]

Throughout spirituals, such images of blind people and people with disabilities are used to highlight both the limitations of human life in a fallen world and the transcendent possibilities engendered by the coming of Jesus.

In its representation of Jesus's encounters with the dispossessed, among whom the physically impaired were no doubt disproportionately represented, the Bible offers an image of Christ as the ultimate "great emancipator." In other words, he came to bring salvation to those most obviously and egregiously impacted by the forces of evil. Such Old Testament passages as "Thou shall not curse the deaf nor put a stumbling block before the blind" (Leviticus 19:14), or "Cursed be he that maketh the blind to wander out of the way" (Deuteronomy 27:18), offered succor far beyond their metaphorical engagement with disability. Not surprisingly, Jesus's strongest appeal for those slaves who accepted Christianity was as a savior particularly willing to attend to those who had been overlooked by the working of society's ameliorative processes. Zan Holmes observes that "the Jesus who invites us to worship is the same Jesus who proclaimed in his first sermon, as recorded in Luke 4:18–19":

> The Spirit of the Lord is upon me,
> because he has anointed me to bring good news to the poor.

He has sent me to proclaim release to the captives
and recovery of sight to the blind,
to let the oppressed go free,
to proclaim the year of the Lord's favor.[7]

The emancipatory perspective reflected in such passages found its musical transmutation in spirituals in which the singers proclaimed such sentiments as,

Children, we shall be free
When the Lord shall appear.
Give ease to the sick, give sight to the blind,
Enable the cripple to walk;
He'll raise the dead from under the earth,
And give them permission to talk.[8]

As such passages indicate, when transcendence is referenced in the spirituals, it is usually as an acknowledgment of a condition in which even the possibility of the redressing of the subject's grievances as the result of his or her own personal agency is unthinkable, un-Christian, and—for slaves always mindful of the powerful forces committed to maintaining their enslavement—unwise.

Sandra Ruconich and Katherine Standish Schneider suggest that "although Christian denominations may differ in their views of blindness or their interpretations of blindness-related biblical text, a common thread of compassion for and support of persons who are visually impaired typifies Christianity."[9] While compassion may indeed reflect one strand of Christianity's scriptural engagement with sightlessness, the reality of biblical consideration of blind people is in fact much more complex, and this complexity is reproduced in black spirituals. Throughout the Bible, the less compassionate side is revealed by the frequency with which blind people and other disabled are presented as the bearers of misfortunes whose symbolic force positions them on the negative side of a punitive binary. Despite the advances in sensitivity that have been made over the years, the idea that blindness and other disabling conditions should be acknowledged as ethically neutral components of human life has not played a consistently positive role in Christian engagement with physical difference.

Although references to blindness occur throughout both the Bible and the texts of the spirituals, the most significant individual blind figure in black spiritual and, later, gospel music is the man known as Blind Bartimus. The story of Bartimus forcefully reflects the dynamics of recognition and repudiation that characterize the spirituals' attempt to "think" disability. It is in fact this story's exemplary presentation of these forces that may help to explain why it became so popular with spiritual and gospel singers and was regularly rediscovered and refashioned as new generations of performers came to the music. A version of the Bartimus story recorded by the group the Harps of Melody recounts the tale as follows:

> In my God's Bible, in the Book of James,
> Christ were healing the crippled and the lame.
> He went to the poor in the need of bread,
> Healing the sick and raising the dead.
> He passed by a man that could not see.
> The man was blind; he was blind from birth,
> Tell me that his name was Blind Bartimus.
>
> Chorus:
> Well, Old Blind Bartimus stood on the way.
> Well, Blind Bartimus stood on the way.
> Well, Old Blind Bartimus stood on the way,
> Crying, "Oh Lord, have mercy on me."
>
> When Bartimus saw that the Lord was nigh
> Fell on his knees and began to cry.
> "Oh thou man of Galilee,"
> Crying "Great God almighty, have mercy on me."
> Cried "Oh Lord, Mary's baby.
> Oh Lord, Son of David.
> Oh, Lord, bleeding lamb.
> Oh my Lord, oh Bethlehem."
>
> Chorus:
>
> Then my God, he stopped, he looked around.
> Then he saw Blind Bartimus on the ground.
> Then he touched his eyes with the palm of his hand.
> Blind Bartimus saw like a natural man.
> He cried "Thank God, Mary's baby.
> Thank God, Son of David.

Thank God, bleeding lamb.
Oh, thank God, oh Bethlehem."[10]

The particulars of Bartimus's story as they were incorporated into the framework of African American religious music provide a striking example of the ambivalence with which blind people were viewed by those looking for signs of spiritual worth and worthlessness. As Gabriel Farrell makes clear, "While Bartimaeus expressed a universal hope for the restoration of sight, it must not be overlooked that when Jesus came his way he was sitting by the gate begging."[11]

If Jesus's willingness to heal blind people and other disabled individuals revealed his awareness of them as figures worthy of his concern, blindness more generally functioned as a marker of God's disfavor and spiritual unworthiness. Reflecting this "scapegoating" dynamic, the image of stasis and passivity that one finds in the story of Bartimus, as well as in such spirituals as "Blind Man Lying at the Pool," suggests that any form of active self-assertion by a blind or disabled person, indicating that they considered themselves already worthy of salvation despite their impairment, could be read as an un-Christian failure to respect the essentially "fallen" order of things.

The complex image of blindness and blind people in an African American spiritual tradition that regularly adapted and redacted well-known white hymns for the purpose of black expressivity is especially interesting when one considers that "the world's most prolific writer of hymns" was herself blind. Fanny J. Crosby (1820–1915) was the most significant of a cadre of white female hymnists who emerged during the late eighteenth and nineteenth centuries. Jane Stuart Smith and Betty Carson note that "the nineteenth century witnessed the phenomenon of women assuming a place of primary importance among hymn writers of the church."[12] In fact, for a significant number of disabled white Christian women whose impairments prevented them from enacting the conventional narratives of wife and mother, the writing of hymns and religious poetry became the kind of default option that blues singing was for blind Southern black men. Fanny Crosby was the best-known and most prolific of these women, and it has been estimated that her published output under her own name and dozens of pseudonyms consisted of almost eight thousand hymns, including such well-known works as "Blessed Assurance," "Pass Me Not, O Gentle Savior," "Jesus, Keep Me Near the Cross," and "Jesus Is Tenderly Calling You Home."[13] Upon her death, an obituary in the *Nashville Tennessean and American* asserted, "It is not much to say that this blind writer of songs has touched and chastened and cheered more hearts than any man or woman who ever lived in America."[14]

Like the most successful of the blind singers and songwriters who followed her, much of Fanny Crosby's personal and professional appeal could be attributed to the fact that throughout her life she was acutely aware of the potentially alienating force of her blindness in a world in which almost everyone else could not only see but could see her. Accordingly, Crosby's persona evolved into one perfectly in keeping with the expectations and fears of the sighted congregants who would most often be singing her songs. However, even when her hymns failed to reference blindness with any explicitness, those songs that Crosby published under her own name were given added spiritual force by her status as one of the world's few truly famous blind people.[15]

Although no blind African American gospel singer or songwriter ever achieved recognition comparable to Fanny Crosby's worldwide fame, it is telling that one of the foundational texts in the tradition of African American gospel music owes its provenance to an image of what could be seen, with very little irony, as an extension of Crosby's "blind faith." As African American culture moved beyond the world that had inspired the spirituals, secular influences began to impact the world of church music. These influences gave rise to the self-consciously hybridized form of "gospel." Correspondingly, the image of blindness in the world of black religious song changed.

In Lucie E. Campbell's "Something Within," which is generally believed to be the first gospel song published by an African American woman, the sighted Campbell established a complex engagement with blindness that would be maintained and extended by blind African American performers themselves as gospel displaced spirituals as the predominant form of black religious musical expression. In an account of the songwriter's encounter with the blind street singer Connie Rosemond, who inspired the song, Campbell's biographer, Reverend Charles Walker, wrote:

> There sat Connie Rosemond, playing hymns and spirituals, as was his custom. It was winter—cold, damp, rainy. Mr. Rosemond's feet were wrapped in burlap bags as he sat and played. Some of the neighborhood men came out of the bar and listened to the musician

play and sing. One of them called to Mr. Rosemond . . . "Hey Connie! I'll give you five dollars to play 'Caledonia' or some other blues," and Mr. Rosemond replied, "Oh, no, I can't do that." The man's partner taunted him. Connie Rosemond stood his ground and responded again, "I can't do that; all I know is that there is something within."[16]

After witnessing Rosemond's unshakeable adherence to Christian principle, Campbell was inspired to write the famous song that asks,

> Have you that something, that burning desire?
> Have you that something, that never doth tire?
> Oh, if you have it that Heavenly fire
> Let the world know there is something within.

> Chorus:
> Something within me, that holdeth the reins;
> Something within me that banishes pain;
> Something within me, I cannot explain
> All that I know, there is something within.[17]

As with many of Fanny Crosby's lyrics, in "Something Within" it is the absent presence of blindness that generates both the song's pathos and its "universality." Despite the fact that Campbell had Rosemond himself premier the song at the 1919 National Baptist Convention, blindness as such is not referenced in the song's lyrics. Instead, it is the inchoate "something within" that grounds the singer's faith.

In his consideration of blindness in the tradition of black religious music, Luigi Monge asserts that "religious texts must clearly convey a redeeming message, therefore, unsighted sacred singers usually ignore their blindness, avoiding any reference to it. When they want to deal with it, they do so through generally rare but sometimes massive statements of God's healing power."[18] Monge then states, "Less frequently, they counterbalance their neglect of sightlessness by thematically developing a very personalized dialogue with god on the subject."[19] It is in fact this second option that was most frequently explored by blind performers who self-consciously positioned both themselves and their sightlessness in the gospel mainstream. Indeed, this personalized position gave these performers access to highly particularized modes of spiritual display and validation *as* blind people. The emphasis shifted from the spirituals' focus on biblical figures and miraculous resightings of the sightless to a re-counting, often by blind performers themselves, of the particulars of their condition as people who were both impaired and worthy.

Horace Boyer writes, "Gospel practitioners seem to agree that gospel music means 'good news' and that good news must come through the lyrics."[20] As a bearer of this "good news," gospel music was much more straightforwardly optimistic and celebratory than the more past-and-present-oriented lyrics of the spirituals. Therefore, not surprisingly, references to blindness in gospel songs written and performed by sighted singers are, as Monge points out, comparatively rare. Still, by subtly rewriting aspects of the tradition of religious black music, the most influential blind gospel singers managed to establish a more blind-friendly site within the world of black religious music. This site did not depend upon or extend the censorious and denaturalizing image of blindness as punishment that was created when sightlessness was referenced by sighted singers as a means of indicating their progress along a continuum of salvation and spiritual worth.

Alternatively, a significant number of the songs written or adapted by blind gospel performers address the ways in which, as individuals, they experienced, failed to experience, or refused to experience their visual impairment as an insurmountable obstacle in their attempts to live godly lives. Rather than asking the Lord to relieve them of the burden of impairment, more often these singers made it clear that they were just as willing as the sighted to toil in the vineyard and be granted their reward in the afterlife with the other saints. For instance, undoubtedly attracted to the dramatic potential of the song's lyrics when performed against the backdrop of both their visual impairment and their obvious spiritual commitment, the blind singers Arizona Dranes, Mamie Forehand, and Blind Willie Johnson all recorded versions of the classic gospel song "Bye and Bye We're Going to See the King." When performed by these blind singers, this song took on an even more heightened sense of eschatology and transcendence than when it was sung by the sighted. For those listeners for whom the impact of the song's lyrics might have become dulled through familiarity, the effect of hearing these blind singers insert themselves as active agents into the narrative of transcendence that the song details was undoubtedly both thrilling and unnerving.[21] The implication was that blind singers, rather than asking for a miraculous healing, were willing to forego the visual pleasures of this world for the privilege of looking upon their maker's face in their and his own due time.

Ironically, the racist effects of segregation that had generated the excessive levels of blindness in black communities in the early decades of the twentieth century may also have facilitated the recording of both blind and sighted black gospel artists and underpinned their greater investment in creating a more user-friendly image of Christian faith. The fact that gospel did not provide as strong a framework for articulations of disability as a negative condition as the spirituals had can to some extent be attributed to the music's generative relationship with the forces of technological modernity. James R. Goff Jr. indicates, "In an age when most southern blacks lacked access to rural electrification and when radio stations catered to the predominantly white market, inexpensive phonographs provided a unique opportunity for budding professional singers to share their talents."[22] Accordingly, in gospel songs, the coming good days that the word "gospel" itself proclaims are rendered with a sense of immediacy grounded in the more dynamic musical backings that modern audiences demanded.

The most influential and best-selling of these early singers was Blind Willie Johnson (ca. 1900–1949). Exclusively devoted to religious music, Blind Willie Johnson was known for the quiet determination with which he approached both his life and his short-lived recording career. In fact, it was Johnson's recognition of singing as both his Christian mission and his job that would lead to his death. Sherry Dupree and Herbert Dupree recount the story:

> In 1949, his house at 1440 Forest Street burned. He and his wife Angeline and their children got out safely, losing his guitar and furnishings. The house was filled with water. His wife spread newspaper over the wet bedding, and they slept in the house that night. Johnson, in his sleep, turned over onto the soaked mattress. He was sick the next day, yet he went out singing on the streets to earn money. His wife tried to get him into the hospital, but he was not admitted because he had no money. One week later, he died with pneumonia.[23]

Although there were more continuities than differences between Johnson's music and that of both the country blues singers and the emerging culture of gospel music, his work has consistently—and, I believe, mistakenly—been read as being somehow "other" to the traditions of both country blues and early gospel. Certainly, Johnson's blindness has made

Blind Willie Johnson, 1897–1945.
Courtesy of John Tefteller and Blues Images.

this attribution of otherness much easier than it would be if his blindness itself did not function so readily as a marker of premodernity. It is this "difference" that has grounded Johnson's ability to function for many as a perfect signifier of folk authenticity and expressive primitivism. Like a blind Robert Johnson, Willie Johnson embodied an essential unknowableness that has made it particularly easy to construct images of him that both rely on and mystify the cultural and physical particulars of his life and work. Mary Wilds observes: "He is a particularly elusive performer in that he left no thoughts of his own behind. There are no known interviews, no autobiographies; only his songs."[24]

In the years since his death, the most discussed of Johnson's songs, and the one that has contributed most to the mystification of the relationship between his blackness and his blindness, is "Dark Was the

Night, Cold Was the Ground." Over the more than six decades since its release, this work, which has been described as "a largely wordless monody of moans accompanied by a restless, singing slide," has been accorded such culturally skewed attention that in the context of this study, these readings are worth considering at length.[25] As I will argue later, it was the specifying wordiness of a song like Blind Gary Davis's "There Was a Time That I Went Blind" that placed it outside the mainstream of black spiritual and gospel music for many cultural purists. Alternatively, it is the wordlessness of Johnson's song that has made it especially susceptible to validation as a singularly authentic "sounding" of both blackness and blindness as markers of some kind of primary ontological "difference" between blacks and whites and between the sighted and the blind.

Critical readings of Johnson's song provide particularly clear cases of the problems that can ensue when the cultural and conceptual base(s) that generated both the spirituals and gospel music are replaced by narratives that give undue or inappropriate prominence to either blindness or blackness as explanatory categories. For instance, after soberly suggesting that in "Dark Was the Night, Cold Was the Ground," the "melodic and harmonic motion speaks of pre-blues and non-blues sounds, of the mono-chromatic harmony of some early song, and the instinctive dissonance of so-called primitive musicians," Allen Lowe feels free to avail himself of a startling degree of creative license and proclaim that "only a Black singer, made motherless as a child, then rendered sightless by random irrational adult violence, condemned to live and wander in the most desolate reaches of the rural South, and probably subject to waking nightmares of searing psychological heat as well as terrifying night visions of hell and damnation, could have sung this."[26]

What hyperbolic assertions of the absolute singularity of Johnson's recording fail to recognize is that this type of wordless song has a long history in black musical expression. In fact, hums, moans, and other types of wordless singing occupy a foundational position in African American religious music.[27] The failure of critics like Lowe to recognize both the brilliance of Johnson's recording and its straightforward relation to the tradition of African American religious music (and of other religious communities that have practiced forms of "lining out") is enabled by the ease with which Johnson's blindness can be used to ground a narrative that positions the song as the sounding of both blindness and blackness as states of literally unspeakable anguish.

Despite the advance that the work of Blind Willie Johnson and other early folk and gospel singers represents over the often punitive represen- tations of blindness in the spirituals, the engagement with blindness as a lived condition that one finds in the work of blind gospel and religious performers could become problematic in different ways as these per- formers became more fully entangled in the world of professional enter- tainment. This potential is made clear by the most explicit and probably best-known song dealing with blindness from the perspective of a African American performer, Reverend Gary Davis's (1896?–1972) "There Was a Time That I Went Blind." In one version of this classic work, Davis sings:

> It was a time when I went blind.
> Was the darkest day that I ever saw.
> Was the time when I went blind.
>
> Lord, I cried the whole night long.
> Crying, oh Lord, won't you tell me how long?
> Am I to be blind always?
>
> Lord, I wished I could see again.
> I wished I could see again.
> If I could see, how happy I would be.
> I wished I could see again.
>
> Lordy, nobody knows like me.
> At [*sic*] the trouble I do see.
> I'm away in the dark, got to feel my way.
> Lordy, nobody cares for me.
>
> Lord, it's hard I have to be blind.
> I'm away in the dark and I have to believe.
> Lord it's hard I have to be blind.
>
> Lordy, nobody knows like me.
> Since I lost my sight, I lost my friends.
> Now there's nobody is a friend to me.
>
> My friends turned their back on me.
> 'Cause I'm away in the dark and I cannot see.
> Yes, they turned their back on me.
>
> Lordy, nobody cares for me.
> 'Cause I'm away in the dark and I cannot see.

Lordy, nobody cares for me.

Lord, my way seems so hard.
Lord, I'm blind, I cannot see.
Says, I'm away in the dark, got to feel my way.
Lord, and my way seems so hard.

It was a time when I went blind.
Was a time when I went blind.
Was the dreadfulest day that I ever seen.
Was a time when I went blind.

Lordy, nobody knows like me.
At [*sic*] the trouble I do see.
You ought all to realize that you got the good sight.
You ought to know that it's a good thing to have.

You can see, it's the truth.
You can see, I mean you can see.
You can see everything coming to you.
It was a time when I went blind.

Most striking about Davis's text as a personalized extension of the
tradition of African American religious song is how easily the singer's
presentation of himself as someone deserving of special attention and
even pity can be considered indicative of an almost hubristic self-con-
cern alien to both spiritual and gospel music's status as modes of collective enunciation. As a contribution to a salvific discourse, Davis's song
blatantly compromises the sense of what Glenn Hinson calls "devotional
equality" that characterizes black religious services.[28] Because even in the
black community, blindness was not a condition that more than a small
percentage of the members of any congregation would be personally ex-
periencing, it is difficult to imagine a song like "There Was a Time That
I Went Blind" being received as anything other than a plea for special
consideration. In fact, it is only the spoken extrapolations that the singer
sharply directs at his sighted auditors that prevent the song from collapsing into complete monological self-absorption. These asides complicate
the flow of the narrative and may in fact indicate Davis's awareness of
how potentially alienating so personal an account of the experience of
blindness might be for both Christian and secular audiences. Blind Gary
Davis's willingness to offer such a starkly personalized expression of

blindness as a distressing personal condition may reflect the fact that, unlike the best-known blind men in the world of mainstream gospel music, the Blind Boys of Mississippi and the Blind Boys of Alabama, Davis almost always worked alone. Once in 1964, when introducing the song to an audience comprised primarily of UCLA students, Davis began by distancing himself from both the song and the condition that had inspired it, while simultaneously acknowledging his new position in the increasingly youth-driven world of popular entertainment: "Now I want to sing you a song that people are always after me to sing. I hardly ever sing it but I hardly ever think to sing about my condition either."[29]

Interestingly, as a song about his "condition," "There Was a Time That I Went Blind" probably did not reflect Davis's experience with any real exactness. Although he sometimes seemed to deliberately confuse the issue, Davis was most likely significantly visually impaired at birth and then rendered completely blind by medical mistreatment while still a young child. Despite the song's title, typically the experience of becoming blind in a day, which "There Was a Time That I Went Blind" recounts, would be that of "being blinded," not that of "going blind." In fact, as an exploration of his "condition," Davis's song blurs the actual distinctions among "being blinded," "becoming blind," and "being blind." Despite its apparent lack of realism as a "true" rendering of blindness and blinding as either emotional or physical events, the narrative presented in "There Was a Time That I Went Blind" does masterfully reflect the imaginings of many sighted people when they attempt to conceive of blindness as a lived condition. As Hector Chevigny and Sydell Braverman write, "The sighted person trying to imagine the blind man's life thinks of it as if each day were a duplicate of the first one; as if the frustrations then encountered present themselves anew and with the same emotional values they first carried, and as if the capacity to solve the problems never increased."[30]

When considering the personal conditions that might have given rise to Davis's crafting of "There Was a Time That I Went Blind," it is perhaps best to imagine the song as a piece that, rather than being designed to provide spiritual enlightenment, was a strategic component of Davis's career as a street singer. This was a role that Davis performed on the streets of Harlem for more than twenty-five years, in conjunction with his role as one of the premier figures in the folk revival of the late 1950s and 1960s. For blind performers, street singing was always in uneasy tension with the image of the blind beggar, an image and stereotype that, not surprisingly, most blind people actively disdain. As one of the most popular figures in the folk revival and a legendary street performer, Davis was particularly adept at adjusting to the demands of different audiences. However, *as* a street singer, Davis was faced with the tricky task of "presenting" himself to and for sighted passersby as a man who was not only blind, gifted, and near the end of his life somewhat famous, but also still poor enough to be on a street corner singing for change.

Although Davis's situation was certainly atypical, over its entire range, the world of religious music is one in which the relationship between payment and performance is only covertly recognized. Therefore, the status of the performers in this world as entertainers, and often surprisingly poor ones, is rarely explicitly acknowledged by either the artists themselves or their fans. This notion of the artist as a saint, someone in the world but not fully of it, may help to explain why it is gospel music that has accommodated the only blind African American woman to achieve a significant degree of popular recognition. This was the spellbindingly intense gospel singer-composer-pianist Juanita Arizona Dranes (1904–57).[31] Robert Darden describes Dranes's impact on the world of black gospel: "While she only recorded thirty sides for the OKeh label between 1924 and 1928, the combination of her electrifying singing and her thumping, rhythm-fused piano playing made her a much in-demand artist at black churches and revivals throughout the country."[32] The very forces that made secular music a somewhat disreputable arena for women legitimated Dranes and other female singers as figures in the gospel world. This was especially true of women affiliated with the Church of God in Christ.[33] The musical openness of this denomination provided Dranes with a space in which she could express her gifts without facing the criticism to which, as a woman, she would no doubt have been subjected had she tried to forge a career in secular music.[34]

From the inception of gospel music, both women and blind singers and musicians like Dranes were respected and even venerated figures in this world.[35] In fact, one of the most significant indicators and aftereffects of the disabling conditions that disproportionately affected African Americans in the first three decades of the twentieth century was the phenomenon of blind singing quartets.[36] Although only two groups of blind singers managed to achieve national success, "one of the most familiar sights of gospel concerts in the 1950s was five or six blind men, each with his hand on the shoulders of the man in front, being led by a sighted man to the performance space."[37] Like blind country blues singers, blind gospel groups fared badly with the rise of electric instrumentation. However, over the long run, they weathered the storm much better because, unlike in the world of secular music, gospel concerts usually were and still are less dependent on one or two superstar performers or groups to provide a full evening of entertainment. Therefore, even when their basic appeal had waned, blind gospel groups could still survive as respected parts of the "caravan."

The most notable and long-lasting of the blind quartets were the Blind Boys of Mississippi and the Blind Boys of Alabama. Tellingly, these groups emerged into real prominence at the moment in the 1940s and through the 1950s and 1960s when the Jubilee style of gospel singing was giving way to the "hard" style that would grow to dominate the form. This transformation would hasten the movement of gospel from its "natural" home in small churches to its more lucrative "house-wrecking" presentation in tents and arenas.[38]

Without doubt, one of the most legendary of these house wreckers was Archie Brownlee, the original lead singer of the Blind Boys of Mississippi. Formed when the original members, Lawrence Abrams, Archie Brownlee, Joseph Ford, Sam Lewis, and Lloyd Woodard, were students at Piney Wood School for the Blind in Piney Wood, Mississippi, the group was first recorded singing secular songs in field recordings for the Library of Congress. Soon, however, its members committed themselves to gospel music and, after a brief stint as the Jackson Harmoneers, changed their name to the Five Blind Boys of Mississippi. Later, as a response to the emergence of the Blind Boys of Alabama, they became the Original Five Blind Boys of Mississippi. For decades, the Blind Boys of Mississippi would be counted among the premier performers in the world of gospel music, and Brownlee became one of the most influential figures in the evolution of gospel performance as an art. Robert Darden reports that "in the throes of a particularly strong manifestation of the Holy Spirit, the completely blind Brownlee would miraculously rush about the stage and sometimes down the aisles. One awestruck observer once reported, 'I seen him at Booker T. Auditorium jump *all* the way off that balcony, down on the floor—*blind*! I don't see how in the world he could do that. People would just fall out all over the house.'"[39] As this statement indicates, the unease elicited by a blind performer—an unease that few sighted people ever manage to fully conquer—was transformed into excitement and wonder by the uniqueness of seeing blind men display such dynamic and seemingly unconstrained physicality. This alone might be enough to keep an audience member's attention raptly glued to the stage.

It is important, however, to consider the possibility that the performative dynamism of blind gospel singers like Brownlee may out of necessity have been as strategic as it was expressive. Ray Allen remarks of gospel performers in general, "The best lead singers possess the ability to read their audiences," and there are certainly few conditions that render an audience as unreadable as blindness would seem to do.[40] Their need to rectify this situation may explain why the most noted blind lead gospel singers have been—even for as extroverted an art form as gospel performance—so blatantly exhibitionistic both vocally and physically. By rendering themselves so singularly spectacular, blind gospel singers lessened the likelihood that their audiences would attend to the kinds of casual distractions that the singer's blindness would prevent him from recognizing and addressing.[41]

Despite the groundbreaking work of the Blind Boys of Mississippi, it was the Blind Boys of Alabama who fundamentally broadened the parameters of gospel expressivity and modernized the image of the blind gospel performer. Formed at the Talladega School for the Negro Deaf and Blind in Alabama in 1939, the Blind Boys of Alabama's willingness, over the decades of their performing life, to explore the space between secular and spiritual artistic expression gave them a transracial appeal that the more traditional Blind Boys of Mississippi never managed to achieve. The Blind Boys of Alabama's movement into general public culture was sparked most notably by the acclaim that the group, especially the lead singer Clarence Fountain, received for their performance as "a group of Oedipuses" in the original 1983 production of the retelling of the Oedipus story in the gospel musical *The Gospel at Colonus*.[42]

Since this production brought them to the attention of mainstream audiences, no other blind performers have demonstrated the capacity and—if truth be told—the necessity for reinvention that the Blind Boys of Alabama have displayed. The widening of their repertoire to include material that has no obvious relation to the tradition of black religious music, and therefore little appeal for black religious audiences, has facilitated this shift. For instance, in recent years they have recorded songs by songwriters as far from this tradition as Tom Waits and Mick Jagger and Keith Richards. These choices—like the fact that in their later incarnations, most of the men on stage performing as the Blind Boys of Alabama have not been blind, whereas in the original group only one mem-

The Blind Boys of Alabama.
Courtesy The Blind Boys of Alabama.

ber was sighted—can be read as a symbolic instance of the general dis-
appearance of blind artists from the world of African American music.
Still, a small number of blind African American performers have
achieved success outside the worlds of blues and gospel music. Ironically,
it is among these performers that we find those artists who have gone on
to become most well-known, widely acclaimed, and generally recognized
as "geniuses."

CHAPTER 4

⸎

Blindness and the Rhetoric of "Genius"
Art Tatum, Rahsaan Roland Kirk, and Ray Charles

When blind performers have become prominent as jazz or rhythm and blues performers, they have had to face both the negative and the positive implications and effects of cultural narratives that position them as "exemplary exceptions" more often than their peers in more folk-based forms. Because of the decreasing rates of blindness over the last four decades, it has become increasingly difficult for modern audiences to relate blind performers to the narratives of "ordinariness" that characterized the cultural reception of performers like Blind Tom and the blind blues and gospel singers. With Tom, it was the narrative of him as a typically unassimilable black man; with the singers, it was that of ordinary black men facing particularly challenging versions of the difficulties that all black men faced. Now, however, their very rarity—in the wake of the decline in blindness in the African American community and in the West in general—and the expansion of career possibilities for blind people have contributed to the consistent characterization of these performers as "exceptions" and "geniuses."

Three of the performers whose lives and music best reveal this shift are the jazz artists Art Tatum and Rahsaan Roland Kirk and the rhythm and blues legend Ray Charles. Despite their differences, these artists are united by the ways in which, over the course of their careers, the historical and personal singularity of their visual impairment(s) has been placed in relation to specifically "modern" narratives of black musical accomplishment: early jazz in the case of Tatum, post-bebop jazz for Kirk, and gospel and early R & B for Charles. Each of these performers had to fashion and legitimate an individualized image of himself in relation to an emerging form of black-driven musical expression, and not primarily to the cultural workings of white racism or to the existence of a cadre of blind performers tilling the same musical soil.

This change in the characterization of blind performers developed primarily as a response to the rise during the 1920s of jazz as an artistically and commercially validated post-minstrel space for African American performers in American popular music. Because it was more difficult for blind people to negotiate the urban environments that gave rise to the form, there were far fewer blind jazz musicians than there were performers who functioned in the worlds of blues and gospel music. Also, as with the "classic blues" singers, stylishness and at least some pretension to urbanity were, from the start, essential aspects of jazz culture. Therefore, black jazz audiences, often consisting of Northern blacks and the more affluent, ambitious, or desperate refugees from the South, were among those least likely to want to be reminded of the conditions that blind performers seemed to symbolize or to maintain an emotional connection to that past, for which country blues had served as a soundtrack.

By the time jazz and, later, rhythm and blues began to displace folk blues as the most popular forms of dance music for black audiences, access to better health services and information had significantly reduced the number of blind African Americans. Although there was still a drastic shortage of both black doctors and white doctors willing to attend to the health needs of African Americans, medical conditions for blacks in the South had improved enough to at least lessen the number of new cases of blindness that were being generated.

Gustavus Stadler observes, in a recent book on the subject, that "a great deal of recent criticism has treated genius skeptically if not with outright hostility, seeing its effects as . . . a 'projection' essentially mystifying the political, economic, and historical factors shaping authorship, or cultural production more generally."[1] Usually, rather than being a straightforward recognition of the exceptional talent of a particular blind artist, the attribution of genius has functioned as a way of countering the deindividualizing narratives to which blind African American performers have frequently been subjected. The circulation of the notion of the performer as "genius" has been especially common in the world of jazz. James Lincoln Collier writes, with only slight exaggeration, "Virtually every jazz musician able to hold his instrument properly has at one time or another been described as a genius."[2]

However, even in a world in which the attribution of genius was so common, perhaps no other jazz performer has been as consistently ac-

Art Tatum, 1909–56.
Courtesy Cleveland Public Library.

corded that title than the pianist Art Tatum. From the very start of his career, Tatum's unparalleled technical virtuosity brought him lavish praise from almost all quarters of the jazz world. For many of his listeners, Tatum's performances seemed so singular and extraordinary that, like those of his predecessor Blind Tom, they bordered on the uncanny. It is in fact significant that one of the accounts of the emergence of

Tatum's talent reproduces almost exactly the most common account of the appearance of Blind Tom's gift:

> When Art was three, his mother took him along to choir practice. After they returned home, she went into the kitchen to prepare dinner and heard someone fumbling with a hymn on the piano. Assuming that a member of the church had dropped by and was waiting for her to come out of the kitchen, she called out, "Who's there?" No one answered, so she entered the parlor, and there sat three-year-old Art, absorbed in playing the hymn.[3]

There were, however, important differences between the late nineteenth-century world in which Blind Tom moved and the burgeoning world of black musical modernity that welcomed Tatum. In the three decades between Blind Tom's death and Tatum's emergence, black popular music had achieved a degree of cultural autonomy and respectful recognition that enabled more consistent validation of exceptional black artistry, especially when the particulars of that artistry were hard to trace to any aspect of the minstrel tradition itself.

Unlike Blind Tom, Tatum never had to face an ideologically motivated group of naysayers committed to delegitimating his talent as "real."[4] In fact, throughout the writings on Tatum, one finds accounts of performers from both sides of the racial divide who admit to being so stunned by Tatum's virtuosity that they questioned their right to even be musicians. For instance, in one of the most famous stories in jazz history, the legendary and legendarily immodest Fats Waller, supposedly while introducing Tatum, announced to the audience, "Ladies and gentlemen, I play piano, but tonight god is in the house."[5] The fact that one finds so few instances of such flagrant self-flagellation in accounts of the performances of even the most legendary of sighted jazz musicians suggests that something more than Tatum's talent made it possible for his peers and competitors to step aside in recognition of his singular greatness.[6] It is likely that Tatum's extreme visual impairment allowed his contemporaries to position him as an unsurpassable musician simply because they suspected that as a virtually blind man, even one who seemed so well-adjusted to his impairment, he could offer so little competition in most of the other areas of their lives.[7]

In an insightful consideration of Tatum's uniqueness and the various opinions concerning the particular nature of his gift and achievements, Gunther Schuller argues that "in a large measure Tatum's art and his career developed parallel to but not really as a part of the jazz mainstream. . . . For Tatum was artistically a loner, not only in the sense that he spent the major part of his career as a solitary soloist . . . but also in the sense that he always stood apart from any major stylistic trends."[8] While this is true, Schuller does not address the aspects of Tatum's life as a blind man that may have given rise to this apartness. He does not consider the possibility that this solitary position may reflect the fact that Tatum's ability to function independently, as an almost blind man in the highly communal world of 1930s and 1940s jazz, was much more limited than he would admit, perhaps even to himself.

Ultimately, it was Tatum's lateral position in relation to the jazz mainstream that grounded the critiques of those most willing to, if not swim, at least paddle against the tide of acclaim that usually greeted his performances. The resistance to Tatum voiced by the few critics who publicly denied his greatness, or at least the extent of it, was usually expressed as a specific engagement with the singularity of his style and the lack of progress that they observed as the years passed. Generally, these critics questioned the "unchallenging" repertoire of standards to which Tatum consistently returned and the increasingly predictable interpretive choices that they felt he made when engaging these works. For instance, one of the earliest and highest-profile figures to inveigh against Tatum's genius was André Hodeir.[9] According to Hodeir, more often than his supporters would admit, Tatum's performances devolved into a "formless torrent in which new ideas pop up only infrequently."[10] Even at their harshest, however, these critical comments were usually offered after an acknowledgment of the critic's general admiration for Tatum as a man and as a gifted, if not consistently forward-thinking musician.

If Tatum was not as musically adventurous or up-to-date as his critics desired, this conservatism may have reflected the fact that the challenges he faced in negotiating the jazz world with the level of independence that he displayed were far greater than most of his contemporaries realized. The fact that Tatum managed to become so successful without the corporate structure of support and the ready access to paid helpers that contributed to the professional longevity of later performers like Ray Charles and Stevie Wonder may to a great extent be traced to the fact that throughout his life he maintained such a significant degree of residual vision. Because his residual vision was so great, Tatum was not ac-corded and did not seek the special consideration that is routinely made available to the completely blind.

It can in fact be very difficult for the sighted to understand how great a functional difference there is between Tatum's position—having what was estimated to be approximately one-eighth of normal vision—and be-ing either completely blind or having a degree of vision that falls within the normal range. Orrin Keepnews observes, of Tatum's response to his visual impairment, "He took pains to demonstrate how much he could do for himself unaided: he delighted in any situations that enabled him to participate as an equal or even to have an advantage over normally sighted people."[11] Because of his residual vision, passing for sighted was much more of a "living" issue for Tatum than it was for most of the bet-ter-known blind musicians. Because of Tatum's ability to pass for sighted, there are many admirers of his work, even today, who are completely un-aware of the fact that his visual impairment was so severe. As an almost blind man, Tatum's performance of the role of sighted person certainly entailed a degree of effort that no doubt prevented him from simultane-ously performing the role of creatively evolving jazz genius with the in-tensity or flair of his sighted contemporaries like Charlie Parker and Thelonious Monk or his blind successor Rahsaan Roland Kirk.

Still, despite his skill at "passing," inevitably Art Tatum had to accept the fact that certain activities were beyond the functional parameters of his visual competence. For instance, Tatum was one of the first of the ma-jor blind African American musical performers to come of age at a time when access to an automobile and the ability to drive were becoming pri-mary social markers of independent manhood and cultural citizenship for American men of all ethnicities.[12] Tanya Titchkosky writes that "see-ing is a cultural achievement surrounded by a set of culturally specific val-ued practices"; one of the cultural achievements most dependent upon the ability to see is driving a car.[13] Although the inability to drive is one of the factors of their lives that blind people most often lament, the fact that Tatum was not completely blind may actually have exacerbated his lifelong and almost obsessive irritation with the fact that he could not see well enough to drive. According to James Lester, "The newly invented au-tomobile was a powerful symbol of independence for him, and the futile impulse to drive one popped up repeatedly in his life."[14]

Such a desire to prove his manliness—to deny the association of blindness with something less than full manhood—may also have been one of the underlying reasons for Tatum's career-long investment in the late-night "cutting contests" at which he was famously competitive and adept. Beyond the musical battles in which more often than not he prevailed, Tatum's affinity for after-hours clubs may also have reflected the fact that in these familiar spaces, "the nearly blind man [often] knew every foot and every angle well enough to move about without tension."[15] In these spaces, Tatum could move with the sense of freedom that blind people usually experience only in the privacy of their homes. It is easy to imagine the appeal that these "passing" moments of freedom might have had for someone dealing with the tensions and challenges generated by life as an almost blind man. In these spaces, the only tension that Tatum had to face was that which he could easily alleviate by the superiority of his playing.

The notion that the music that Tatum produced in these after-hours sessions was greatly superior to his recorded work has become a central component in the critical narrative of Tatum's genius. The extravagant claims that have been made for these late-night sessions have generated a "You had to have been there" situation for those who profess to be less than fully convinced of Tatum's genius by the evidence of his recordings. These critics have been rendered incapable of challenging the special insider knowledge of those who were "on the scene" and who have therefore positioned themselves beyond the force of the anti-Tatum critics' deconstructive readings of Tatum's recorded legacy.

If from the start of his career Art Tatum was read as a genius, the multi-instrumentalist Rahsaan Roland Kirk has, alternatively, just as consistently been read as something of a joke. Perhaps no blind African American musical performer has come as close as Kirk to reproducing the relationship between blindness and "freakishness" that characterized Blind Tom Bethune or has had that relationship so freely and negatively referenced in the reception of his work.[16] As Kirk's prominence grew and more conservative figures in the jazz world accepted the fact that not only was he not going to go away, but that he would actually become more outrageous and provocative as time passed, Kirk faced a substantial group of writers and musicians who argued that his music was neither exceptional nor even "real" jazz. They argued that his antimusical antics, political diatribes, and qualitatively inconsistent performances and recordings offered evidence of the degeneration of jazz, rather than of its evolution.

Gene Santoro asserts that "Kirk remains one of the most underval-

Rahsaan Roland Kirk, 1936–77.
Courtesy Cleveland State University Library.

ued and pivotal figures in a field with more than its fair share of the underappreciated."[17] Kirk's relegation to the margins of the contemporary pantheon of "great" jazz musicians reflects the ambivalence that his commitment to being both entertaining and politically outspoken generated. He arrived on the scene at a time when jazz was, on the one hand, becoming increasingly positioned as the most creatively significant form of African American "high" culture and, on the other, relegated to the status of a commercial byway in the increasingly corporatized world of 1960s and 1970s popular music. Many listeners and observers felt that Kirk went too far in one direction. while others felt that he went too far in the other. John Kruth writes of Kirk, in his stellar biography *Bright Moments: The Life and Legacy of Rahsaan Roland Kirk,* "He was truly a sight to behold, with his nostrils flaring like a mad bull and his cheeks puffed out like a monstrous chipmunk, pumping air continuously into a strange array of instruments that hung from his body like crazy plumbing or tangled octopus tentacles, all stuck together with masking tape."[18]

If Kirk can be considered a pivotal figure in the world of modern jazz, it could be argued that he occupies that position in relation to a range of musical forms and cultures of the 1960s and 1970s. In fact, Kirk's very eclecticism allowed him to achieve a degree of popularity with nonjazz audiences that few of his contemporaries managed. The extremity and hyperindividuality of Kirk's stage presence, in conjunction with his blindness, engendered an element of aggressiveness and unpredictability that audiences accustomed to both the simmering but essentially self-contained stance of bop and post-bop jazzmen and the more benign and other-regarding personas of Kirk's blind contemporaries Ray Charles and Stevie Wonder found unsettling.

Much of the resistance to Kirk's actual music may be attributed to the fact that in the post-bop context of the 1960s, the bulk of his work bears little relation to what is usually considered to be the advanced jazz of the period. Instead, like that of Blind William Boone, it is perhaps best read as an aggressively hybridized amalgam of almost all of the musical elements that were at play during the period. For instance, Kirk's penchant for offering relatively untroubled and accessible renditions of popular songs in a period when free jazz and, later, various types of jazz fusion were being heralded as the new thing made him an object of suspicion for avant-gardists. In fact, the melodic and structural straightforwardness of many of Kirk's recordings and compositions often comes as a surprise to those who come to them with preconceived notions of his "eccentricity" and difficulty.

Alternatively, Kirk's rambling political diatribes and often provocative stage manner alienated the neotraditionalists who were beginning to fashion the conservative narrative of jazz as "America's classical music." Kirk's position was that jazz was "Black Classical Music," and he positioned himself as the arbiter and gatekeeper of that tradition. In an unnecessarily precious but acute articulation of the specificity of Kirk's aesthetic, Josh Kun notes, "The removal of both the sound/vision hierarchy and the sound/vision dichotomy is particularly crucial in the context of Kirk because he worked directly within the tradition of African American expressive culture and artistic production, a tradition that, contrary to what many scholars have argued, is defined by the removal of these hierarchies and dichotomies where sound and vision, the aural and the scriptural, have always been interlinked."[19] Despite the suggestiveness of this passage, Kun's collapsing of Kirk's deconstruction of the sound/vision hierarchy into a general notion of this as an aspect of African American expressive culture is problematic. It minimizes the extent to which challenging this hierarchy was in fact one of the strongest markers of Kirk's explicitly politicized militancy as a man who, more than any other African American blind artist, was both self-consciously black and self-consciously blind.

Just as there were a handful of critics who didn't fully accept the narrative of Art Tatum's genius, there were contemporary writers who attempted to create such a narrative for Kirk and to disassociate him from the narratives that positioned him as a freak or a novelty act. The gestures that sparked these narratives included such things as playing two or three horns at once, engaging in marathon sessions of circular breathing in which he would hold a single note for seemingly inhuman amounts of time, and constantly introducing strange and "foreign" instruments into his repertoire. Francis Davis suggests that "writers friendly to Kirk went to great lengths to disassociate him from carny performers with a similar bag of tricks. . . . Kirk's genius was in having it both ways—in knowingly exploiting the sideshow aspects of his act in the cause of musical advancement."[20] Although the extent to which Kirk's music in general actually represented an "advance" over that of his peers is debatable, Davis is certainly correct in his assertion that both the musical and the theatrical aspects of Kirk's performances were far from being the mindless buffoonery that his detractors claimed.[21] Rather than being instances of "clowning" or of eccentricity for its own sake, Kirk's performances were much more often culturally and politically self-conscious expressions of his sense of self as a gifted black man in a "white man's" world, an individual in a world of conformists, and an "unsighted" man in a world in which almost everyone else could see.

Art Tatum's acclamation as a "genius" was generated primarily by his contemporaries' initial response to his astonishing and seemingly unparalleled technical gifts. Further, as I will explore later, recognition and dissemination of the "Genius of Ray Charles" was at its inception little more than a marketing ploy in which the legendarily pragmatic Charles had no particular emotional investment. Kirk, on the other hand, was not at all hesitant to proclaim himself a genius even when very few of his peers were willing to second the claim. This self-confident investment in the value of his difference was reflected in Kirk's unusual willingness, for a blind performer, to suggest that he was, in a musical mode, creatively exploring and sounding the most obvious of these differences—his sightlessness. Kirk often said to his auditors, "Sound is to me what sight is to you."[22]

Following his lead, Kirk's champions have also been much more willing to declare his music to be his way of sounding a world that he could not see than Art Tatum's supporters have been to suggest a generative relationship between Tatum's music and his visual impairment. For instance, the novelist Leon Forrest wrote in his essay "A Journey into the Forest of Roland Kirk Country": "In his attempt to carry everything he sees down the landscape of his Art, Kirk must carry all that is present, all that is ever-green from past wars of survival of black people into today's larger war. All that he can hear; and all that he can see with his 'blinding sight.'"[23] Most attempts to correlate the music of blind performers with some type of expressive particularity that can be traced to their visual impairment have been misguided and reductive. However, the dialectical nature of much of Kirk's music, its alternating but ultimately synthetic currents of pugnacious busyness and seductive calmness, does suggest an attempt by the musician to both render his own complicated nonvisual internal soundscape and to indicate his nonhostile engagement with the soundscape of a visual world that he could not see.[24]

Of all of the African American musical performers who have been placed in the pantheon of "geniuses," Ray Charles is the one of whom we should be most mindful of Robert Mendl's assertion that "'the greatest genius is the most indebted man' and it is the use which he makes of his

Ray Charles, 1930–2004.
Courtesy Cleveland Public Library.

legacy that counts."[25] In the 1950s and 1960s, as access to white popular audiences increased for black performers, African American popular music saw the rise of a group of male singers who represented a turn away from the physicality and cultural markings of performers like Muddy Waters and Howlin' Wolf, toward a less regionalized but still indicatively "black" presentation of masculinity. As a blind but conventionally handsome man—one of the people who in blindness research are sometimes referred to as "the beautiful blind"—Ray Charles was particularly well-positioned to benefit from the shift in taste fostered by the corporate cultures of record companies like Atlantic and Motown. This shift occurred as these companies recognized the commercial possibilities of rhythm and blues and other forms of black music as they were more widely disseminated beyond the African American community and the world of "race" records.[26]

Ray Charles emerged into public culture at the precise moment when a telegenic appearance and image were becoming as important as the quality of a performer's music in determining his or her career prospects. Correlatively, by the late 1940s, the decline in the rates of blindness had made blind people (especially blind black people) much rarer than anyone could have imagined even a few decades earlier. As his fame grew, Ray Charles became one of the few black or blind performers given regular access to television audiences and, thereby, to the normative and legitimating gaze of mainstream white America. As a dual-purpose role model, Charles was faced with the challenge of providing an unthreatening image of both blackness and blindness for audiences who were generally uncomfortable with the former and increasingly unfamiliar with the latter.[27]

Charles's resistance to stereotypical notions of what it meant to be a "blind" person or a blind musician was never extreme enough to cause him to disavow his identity as a blind man, but, like many adventitiously blind people, throughout his life he displayed some degree of what blind activists call "rejection of identification." At its worst, this describes the behavior of "the blind person who will have absolutely nothing to do with any other blind person."[28] Although Charles never went that far, his general resistance to appearing to be too closely aligned with the "idea" of blindness may have played a significant role in generating the energy with which he committed himself to championing the needs of the deaf after he experienced an ear ailment that he feared might threaten his hearing.[29]

Attempts to lessen the negative impact that the sightless eyes of blind people often had on sighted audiences had been common since the public performances of figures like Laura Bridgman, whose eyes were usually covered by silk ribbons when she was presented to the public. It was Charles, however, who—more than any of the artists who preceded him—made sunglasses a standard part of the blind performer's public image. Michael Lydon notes of Charles's first publicity photo that "a re-touch artist painted sunglasses on RC's face. . . . Some people found his eyeless visage disconcerting. Sunglasses worked as an instant, glamorous solution, and thus was born the Ray Charles mask, the pregnant symbol, known around the world, of a sightless singer who cannot be fully seen."[30] Once this "glamorous solution" was in place, a way had to be found to exploit Charles's glamour while preventing him from falling into the cultural nonspace that had entrapped equally handsome blind black men like Al Hibbler. The solution to this problem was to remove Charles from the space of the crooner that Hibbler had tried to occupy and to find a way to positively reference both Charles's blackness and his blindness. In fact, the most telling evidence of Hibbler's limitations as essentially a jazz singer was revealed by Charles's spectacular success only a few years later.

Best known for his work with the Duke Ellington Band, Hibbler had a spotty solo career that demonstrates the difficulty that blind singers had in carving out commercially viable niches for themselves after the heyday of country blues singers like Blind Lemon Jefferson and Blind Blake, when elegance and sexual allure became components as significant for male stage personae as they had been for the classic female singers. Hibbler's failure to find a stable place within black popular music was no doubt exacerbated by the discomfort that the sight of a single blind man standing relatively motionless on stage presented for both jazz and rhythm and blues artists. It was the exploitation of the provenance of his music in the sound and ethos of black gospel, not of guitar-based country blues or 1930s and 1940s big band jazz, that provided Charles with his initial entrée into real prominence and laid the groundwork for the recognition of his "genius."

Although Charles self-consciously distanced himself from the folk tradition of blind bluesmanship, to a limited extent he did attempt to create a genealogy for himself as a musician who happened to be blind. He did this most explicitly by following in the footsteps of another of his heroes, Fats Waller, and positioning Art Tatum as "god," the exemplary instance of pianistic excellence.[31] Charles wrote: "Must say that even later, when I got fairly good at the piano, I knew that I couldn't even carry Art Tatum's shit bucket. The man was alone and no one could touch him."[32] Charles's valorization of Tatum, rather than any of the country blues artists, and his choice of the piano reflected his resistance to the stereotypical notions of blind people and blind musicians to which he had been exposed during his youth: "Now it's important that you understand that there were three things I never wanted to own when I was a kid: a dog, a cane, and a guitar. In my brain, they each meant blindness and helplessness. (Seems like every blind blues singer I'd heard about was playing the guitar.)"[33] Very early in his career, before club owners learned exactly with whom they were dealing, Charles—like the country blues singers who had preceded him—was actually advertised as "Blind Ray Charles." It was, however, the long-established practice, by both sighted and blind musicians, of placing Tatum in that role of exemplar that made referencing him relatively risk-free in terms of positioning Charles as just another blind black musician.

Reflecting the inability of many nondisabled observers to recognize people with disabilities as social agents no more desirous of ethical dispensations than anyone else, commentators, when faced with the more disreputable aspects of Charles's life as his celebrity and iconic status grew, often seemed to be blinded by the light of his blindness. Over the more than five decades of his public life, the media's construction of Ray Charles the man revealed a tendency to consider this most worldly of performers as somehow above the world in which he moved with such obvious authority.[34] For instance, Arnold Shaw wrote of Charles's well-publicized and acknowledged years of heroin addiction, "Not even a bout with drugs (for which the greed of others was totally responsible since he was unable to inject himself) could dim the remarkable creative talent with which he was endowed."[35]

Of course, the notion that Charles was just a helpless pawn caught in the clutches of sighted manipulators who forced him to become a junkie for their own nefarious purposes is counter to the reality of Charles's life as it has been described by both Charles himself and his biographers. In fact, the primary way in which Charles compensated for the extent to which he was dependent on others, in both his personal and his professional life, was by being notoriously demanding and controlling. His biographer David Ritz reports, "To Ray, control was everything—control of his money, his women, his music."[36] The detailed and often bracingly unvarnished recounting of his chemical and sexual adventures that Charles offers in his autobiography serves, in its extremity, to deconstruct the sanctifying rhetoric in the popular press that has at times threatened to overwhelm recognition of Charles's specifically musical artistry, his real "genius."[37]

If, as Albert Murray suggests, a genius is someone "to whom nothing is sacred," the key to Charles's genius was his seamless and, for his detractors, sacrilegiously knowing synthesis of the blues and gospel traditions. Asserting that Charles "treats the gospel of devoted churchgoers as if it were the pop music of Tin Pan Alley," Murray soon emerged as one of the singer's most heated detractors.[38] For such critics, Charles's brazenly obvious rewriting of well-known gospel songs revealed his lack of respect for the cultural integrity of the material that he was appropriating. According to Murray, "When he bootlegs *This Little Light of Mine, I'm Goin [sic] Let It Shine* into his dance-hall version, *This Little Girl of Mine,* the assumption seems to be that the sacrilege can be nullified by sentimentality; but the effect of doing ballroom and honky-tonk steps to such music would have once struck people of both branches of the idiom as being infinitely more offensive than parody."[39] Similarly, when discussing the "churchiness" of some blues instrumentalists, Arthur Lee Williams, a singer interviewed by William Ferris for his book *Blues from the Delta,* said of Charles: "You can hear the same thing in Ray Charles' singing. He used to sing with a blind quarte[t] . . . and you can still hear it in his voice and the way he plays."[40]

The particular resistance to the appropriative gestures that characterized Charles's sound and performances was no doubt exacerbated by the singer's intuitive and seemingly guilt-free recognition of the extent to which those outside of the black church community lacked any real emotional or spiritual investment in the forms that he was using. For white secular audiences, as well as for the less "churchy" African Americans who snatched up his records and flocked to his shows, the liveliness of Charles's music and the pleasure he took in making it served as evidence of the essential "righteousness" of what he was doing. One resistant critic complained: "I have seen whites snap their fingers and dance a jig to Black gospel songs, as if it were another kind of popular secular music. They fail to understand that this musical genre is as sacred as any anthem and is designed not for entertainment but for praise."[41] One could argue, however, that over the course of his career, Charles's fundamental awareness of the sacredness of the tradition that he was adapting was revealed by the fact that, despite his legendary eclecticism, he never recorded a gospel album.

Despite the fact that he became the standard-bearer for the early notion of rhythm and blues as gospel gone bad, in both its vituperativeness and its ultimate futility, the criticism that Charles received mirrored the negative response from the church faithful that gospel singers and songwriters themselves had received during the early days of the music. By the time of Charles's breakthrough into what was for a while an unparalleled degree of transracial success and recognition, increasing numbers of black gospel artists were taking their church-honed skills and rhythms into the world of secular music.[42]

Early in his career, it was Charles's popular success, rather than critical recognition of his syncretizing deployment of black musical traditions, that laid the groundwork for his recognition as something special. In fact, he was not embraced much more enthusiastically by the first generation of blues critics and scholars than he had been by the African American church faithful. In a passage that typifies the often condescending resistance of some blues scholars to Charles's work, Paul Oliver wrote: "A studied exploitation of blues idioms was to be found in the music of Ray Charles. . . . He had not the genius that was claimed for his versatility, but he could undoubtedly put in as convincing a version of *Let The Good Times Roll* as he could *Carry Me Back to Old Virginny.*[43] For writers like Oliver, there seems to have been the suspicion that the particular attention that Charles gained because of his impairment too often drew attention away from the work of both his more stylistically original sighted competitors and his more authentically folkish blind predecessors. Even as self-consciously evenhanded a musicologist as the great Eileen Southern placed Charles outside the black musical mainstream when, after reporting that "the music of Ray Charles defied neat categorization," she concluded that "perhaps his most original contribution to the history of popular music was his fusion of gospel with country-western, as in his album *Modern Sounds in Country and Western Music* (1962)."[44]

Ironically, despite the animus and attention that his success generated, Charles's time as a major hitmaker on the R & B charts was relatively short. Although Charles would never lose his iconic status, as evidenced by his spectacular reemergence as a pop culture icon in the 1990s, after the 1950s the appeal of his music for black audiences would never again be as great as it would become for white Americans and European audiences.[45] By then the sheer brazenness of his hybridized sound had lost most of its novelty. The frequency with which his records reached the R & B charts in the late 1950s and 1960s, and the relatively low positions at which they peaked, indicates that, for black audiences, Charles had become more of a presence than a force at the very moment when he began to sell record numbers of albums to the whites who were discovering "black" music: "His pop hits still became R&B hits, but more as a reflection of their pop success than because of special appeal to the Negro market."[46]

Charles's landmark album *Modern Sounds in Country and Western Music* was released at the very moment when the number of R & B artists who had revealed themselves capable of authoritatively deploying the kind of gospelized R & B that he had pioneered had reached enough of a critical mass to suggest that his talent might not be as singular as it had seemed only a few years earlier. Although other black singers had preceded Charles in melding country and western music with blues and gospel idioms, it was Charles who reaped most of the benefits and was credited by the popular press with this innovation.[47]

To his credit, from the Charles Brown and Nat King Cole imitations with which he began his career through his greatest R & B and country and western successes, Charles himself never denied the essentially mimetic underpinnings of his style. Nor did he apologize for them. In his autobiography, he asserts: "Hell, I was so happy to be able to duplicate things I was hearing around me, I didn't see any problems. And besides, I did my imitations with real feeling. I was doubly proud when I found out I could imitate other singers. Sometimes I came so close that you might confuse me with the original."[48]

When considering the particulars of Charles's synthesizing instincts, one might ask why his supposed lack of originality became such an issue for critics, even though copying the styles of other performers had always been standard practice for apprentice singers and musicians. In fact, such copying could be expected to play an even greater role in the maturation of blind performers, whose engagement with sound as such will necessarily be more intense and, at least initially, mimetic. Much of the answer may be traced to the fact that, despite his straightforward assertion that "I have sense enough to know I am not a genius," Ray Charles, more than any other figure in American popular music, is the artist for whom the concept of "genius" has been most opportunistically incorporated into his professional persona.[49] Charles remarked of the string of "Genius" albums released between 1959 and 1961:

> It wasn't my idea. Calling someone a genius is some heavy shit, and I'd never have used the word in regard to myself. I think I'm pretty good at what I do, but I've never considered myself a genius. . . . I saw it as a high compliment, and I certainly didn't complain. If the

public accepted that, fine. On the other hand, I tried very hard not to let myself feel pressure.[50]

Fittingly, it was the "Genius of Ray Charles" that was decisively consolidated in Charles's posthumously released duets album *Genius Loves Company* (2004). Despite mixed reviews, *Genius Loves Company* went on to become the best-selling album of Charles's career and was awarded eight Grammy awards, including the major awards of album and record of the year.

The success of *Genius Loves Company* was just one component of what could, with very little exaggeration, be called "The Year of Ray Charles." The multiplatinum sales of this recording, coupled with the critical and popular success of *Ray,* the feature-film biography based on Charles's life, and its soundtrack, caught even the most optimistic pop culture mavens by surprise. Troublingly, however, the very extent of the posthumous validation of Ray Charles leads one to wonder about the significance of the fact that the singer's blind and aged body was no longer around to create a counternarrative to the sentimentally reconstructed image that emerged into sharper view, as an apparently endless string of twenty-something hip-hop stars sauntered up to the mike to sing the "genius's" praises during awards season. Arguably, the absence of Charles's own specifically disabled and nonstandard physical reality served to make *Genius Loves Company* and *Ray* simply entertaining cultural documents that, unlike the biopic *Ali* from the previous year, could be enjoyed by the able-bodied casual fan with a sense of pleasure completely untroubled by the presence of the disturbing "thing in itself."

Most obviously, this absence was revealed by the justified and practically universal acclaim that Jamie Foxx received for his performance as Ray Charles.[51] In fact, the very brilliance of Foxx's Oscar-winning enactment of Charles brought to light many of the problems that disability advocates have found in most mainstream theatrical and cinematic depictions of disability.[52] Despite the brilliance of his performance, it was Foxx's exuberantly unimpaired physicality that was inevitably made available for review in the media blitz that Foxx undertook upon release of the film. Finally, in their metonymic leap from the screen to the stage on Oscar night, Jamie Foxx's shining eyes functioned for the unimpaired as a fantastic and essentially utopian enactment of their ultimate wish, a beloved blind man who could not only sing and dance but, finally, do the one thing that really matters—see.

✒️

CHAPTER 5

The Inner and Outer Visions of
Stevie Wonder

One of the things that research on exceptional achievement has made clear is that both geniuses and prodigies are made and not born. In other words, neither the prodigy nor the genius is the result of "natural" processes. Unlike Harriet Stowe's Topsy, you can never say of a prodigy that he or she "jes grew." In the popular imagination, however, few "facts" about African American popular culture have been as taken for granted or seemingly indisputable as the notion that Stevie Wonder was an amazing child prodigy whose talent appeared practically from nowhere and "naturally" evolved into genius. Close examination reveals that the truth is considerably more complicated and much more interesting. Recognition of the particulars of Wonder's development into the legendary performer that he has become can only serve to deepen our appreciation of his achievement. In fact, as often happens with the coding of the talents of black performers as "natural," the notion of Wonder as a child prodigy has only served to mystify the relatively straightforward relationship between his background and early years and the incredible music that he has produced and the remarkable man that he has become over the more than four decades of his life as a public figure.

In a startlingly exact representation of the dynamics of Stevie Wonder's early life and career, Michael J. A. Howe remarks of child prodigies:

According to a romanticised notion of the child prodigy that has been portrayed in a number of novels and films, the typical prodigy is brought up in unpromising circumstances until it is discovered that the child possesses some rare innate gift. Thereupon a wealthy or powerful sponsor arrives on the scene to rescue the *wunderkind*

Stevie Wonder, b. 1950.
Courtesy New York Library for the Performing Arts.

from poverty and make available those opportunities that will enable the young person's special gift to be properly nourished. Thus
armed, the child rapidly becomes a star at the activity at which he or
she excels, and before long is hugely successful, rich and celebrated.[1]

In the African American community, powerful sponsors have not
been particularly abundant. Therefore, relatively few talented youngsters
have been given the opportunity and resources to fulfill their potentially

prodigious possibilities. Despite the attention that Stevland Morris's musical gifts attracted, at their inception they did not seem to be significantly greater than those of any number of musically talented children.[2]

Before being signed to Motown records at the age of nine, Stevie Wonder had established a significant local reputation by performing in local churches and singing for coins on the streets of Detroit. Rather than either the nature or the extent of his gifts, what facilitated Wonder's growth beyond this attention-getting amateurism and into the high level of adolescent and then adult musicianship that he would achieve was his access to the corporate world of Motown and the musical culture that it had engendered in Detroit and was rapidly disseminating to the rest of the world. Wonder himself has remarked on his good luck: "The marriage of myself, Berry Gordy and Motown . . . all of that couldn't have happened at any other place."[3]

In conjunction with the musical culture of Motown, Wonder's talents were also nurtured by that most productive of musical training grounds, the African American church. Over the years, the black church has been a particularly important force in the production of seemingly prodigious musical competencies. Teresa L. Reed astutely points out that "in denominations which value spontaneity, even the youngest of children participate in the church's musical activities, where they learn gospel performance through listening, imitation, and improvisation. Therefore, by the time such a child is a teenager, he or she is already well-versed in the types of musicianship skills that transfer easily into the arena of secular performance."[4] Ironically, it was Wonder's blindness, his "handicap," that gave him access to musical and educational domains well beyond those available to most children of his ethnic and class background and enabled him to develop his talents to their limits.

Like the notion of the "genius" of Ray Charles, the construction of Wonder as a prodigy generally neglects to give any real recognition to the degree to which he benefited from a first-rate musical education, in addition to the musical apprenticeships he served in the church and at Motown. In Wonder's case, this musical training was especially thorough and rigorous because of the relatively advanced state of education for blind people in Michigan at the time and the access to it that Wonder, as a black Northerner, enjoyed. Wonder was given intensive musical training at the Michigan State School for the Blind, as well as supplementary academic work with a private tutor when performing on Motown tours.[5] This tutor, Ted Hull, has reported: "At no other public school in Michigan did every student study orchestra, piano and voice on a daily basis. Along with his private piano lessons, Stevie learned to play both string bass and violin. He learned music composition and chord structure, and was trained in classical music."[6] This technical proficiency and Wonder's familiarity with the formal markers of classical music quickly becomes apparent to anyone who listens to the music he produced once he took over the reigns of his musical productions in the 1970s. This is especially clear in his most ambitious works, *Songs in the Key of Life* and *Journey through the Secret Life of Plants* . . .

Although the congenitally blind rarely display any significant psychological distress in accepting or dealing with their sightlessness, Wonder's seemingly complete "transcendence" of his blindness as a problem became one of the signature components of his public image. The range of options that the young Wonder had as a performer made it even easier for him to forgo any effort to give the particulars and challenges of his life as a blind person any real prominence in his public persona. Wonder has said, "I never really wondered much about my blindness or asked questions about it, because to me, really, being blind was normal; since I had never seen it wasn't abnormal for me."[7] No doubt, however, the relatively privileged life that Motown provided and his access to such a strong educational environment played an added role in the markedly untroubled psychological and, more importantly, professional adjustment that he seems to have made to his blindness from his earliest days.

It is also possible that the diagnostic straightforwardness of Wonder's inability to see may have been a factor. Because he is one of the blind performers whose condition's cause can most easily be pinpointed, Wonder's blindness wasn't really abnormal for anyone. Born two months premature, he spent the first fifty-two days of his life in an incubator. It was this experience that most likely caused him to develop the blinding condition known as retrolental fibroplasia, which would ultimately become "the largest single cause of blindness in children ever recorded in the United States."[8] According to Frederick J. Spencer, "Retrolental fibroplasia was unknown before the 1940s. It was then that aggressive oxygen therapy was started in the treatment of premature infants with respiratory disease. Some of these infants became blind. Research showed that a high oxygen concentration caused a dense fibrous band to replace normal tissue behind the lens."[9] The notion that his blindness was somehow punishment for some kind of original sin—an idea that his contemporary Ronnie Milsap was forced to endure—lost much of its force in a case like Wonder's, where scientific fact could so easily be referenced to demystify his condition.

It is sadly ironic that opportunity rather than disenfranchisement in effect generated the condition of Wonder and children like him. Because African American children who developed retrolental fibroplasia were born in the more urban and metropolitan parts of the country, it may have been more difficult for them to find satisfying social roles as blind people as they grew into adulthood. Frances Koestler points out that "for the most part, cases of retrolental fibroplasia were occurring only in the biggest and most sophisticated medical centers, hospitals that boasted the best in equipment and care. Virtually no cases were reported from rural or suburban hospitals."[10] The same access to the most advanced medical technology that had both caused their condition and saved their lives also provided these children with access to the most advanced training and rehabilitative facilities. Across ethnicities, this training created a cadre of talented young blind men and women who, upon reaching adulthood, existed in numbers far in excess of the accepting occupational roles available to them.[11] Wonder's preadolescent embrace by Motown prevented him from having to face this bleak situation when he reached his twenty-first birthday. This may also help us understand why Wonder has made the essentially symbolic gesture of remaining with Motown throughout his career. James Haskins and Kathleen Benson note, of this relationship: "Corporations are not known for their sense of responsibility, much less for a sense of decency, but Motown took care of Stevie Wonder, and it wasn't the mere protection of an investment. They really did have the best of intentions toward Stevie Wonder, human being."[12]

In his autobiography *To Be Loved: The Music, The Magic, The Memories of Motown,* Motown founder Berry Gordy reports that, although he didn't specifically remember the occasion, he exclaimed to no one in particular, while watching Stevie perform in the studio, "'Boy! That kid's a wonder' and the name stuck."[13] Given the history of physically impaired performers in the entertainment world, the "stickiness" of this name when applied to a young blind black performer who was capable of performing with such proficiency and self-assurance is not surprising. The word "wonder" inadvertently echoes the rhetoric of nineteenth-century freak shows that consistently framed physical disability as "extraordinary." Robert Bogdan points out that, in freak show culture, "wonders" were considered "wonders" "not so much for what they did as for the simple fact that they violated people's expectations of what they could do."[14]

Berry Gordy has described the young Wonder: "Stevie had a cute, mischievous personality and a great sense of humor. His blindness never seemed to bother him; instead he used it as an advantage."[15] In the context of early 1960s popular culture, Wonder's condition may also have been advantageous in other ways. It is telling that it was Wonder who became the first Motown male solo artist to score a number-one pop hit. In her consideration of the commodification of "cuteness" in American popular culture, Lori Merish argues that "the aesthetics of cuteness courts consumer empathy, generating a structure of emotional response that assimilates consumption into the logic of adoption."[16] According to Merish, "cuteness engenders an affectional dynamic through which the Other is domesticated and (re)contextualized within the human 'family.'"[17] For a culture having to adjust to a rising tide of black militancy, what could be cuter and more reassuring than a perpetually smiling little blind black child? At a moment when black men like Martin Luther King Jr. and Malcolm X were legitimating new and more intimidating modes of black masculinity as components of public culture, this renaming or reinventing of Stevland Morris, essentially just another ghetto boy, as "Little Stevie Wonder" (both "little" and a "wonder") served to position him as a black male who had been thoroughly vetted before being brought before the public's gaze.[18]

Because Wonder was little, cute, and blind, he was kept relatively immune from the often viciously competitive culture of early Motown. The way in which the young Wonder could be used by Berry Gordy to reinforce his notion of Motown as a family rather than just a company seems to have been an essential component of Gordy's willingness to invest so much time and so many resources in Wonder, who after his first hit, "Fingertips Part 2," suffered a significant dry spell as a hitmaker.[19] According to Ted Hull, Wonder's private tutor during his teen years, "To most of the Motown musicians, Stevie wasn't a peer. He was a kid, a toy."[20] It was as a toy, a living doll, that Wonder was received both within and outside of Motown until the constraints of this image became too great, and he self-consciously began the difficult process of growing up in public.

Wonder fell back on the musical training that he had received at the Michigan State School for the Blind. It would be his instrumental skills, not his voice, that provided him with a swift line of flight away from the potentially career-killing dynamics of his status as a novelty act and, as an impaired person, his emergence as a handsome, sexually mature, and politically self-aware African American man. Although today Wonder is primarily known as a keyboardist, his use of the harmonica—or, as it is more commonly called in black folk culture, the harp—placed him directly in the line of blues expression that Ray Charles had self-consciously avoided by choosing the piano rather than either the harp or the guitar as his instrument.[21] Wonder's proficiency on what by the early 1960s was a relatively uncommon instrument in mainstream popular music prevented him from being just another kid who could sing. In fact, it was the signifying relationship between Wonder and the blues tradition that his harmonica playing suggested, as well as his identification with Ray Charles as a blind person, that were highlighted in Motown's initial attempts to fashion a readable site for Wonder within black popular culture. By releasing the track "I Call It Pretty Music (But the Old Folks Call It the Blues)" (1962) as Wonder's first single, Motown attempted to position the young singer as both something old and something new, and that something old would be Ray Charles.[22] As the last two blind African American musicians to emerge into general prominence, Ray Charles and Stevie Wonder have been paired in the public imagination for more than four decades.

Long after Charles's breakthrough achievements had been thoroughly assimilated into the soundscape of black popular music and much more consistently groundbreaking artists had appeared on the scene, the rhetoric of Ray Charles as a "genius" was still being used to ground public recognition of his work. It was inevitable that this image would also color the reception of the manchild who seemed to be Charles's most obvious successor. Aaron Fuchs suggests that "the link to Ray Charles was an irresistibly obvious one. Both were blind, black men, and passionate singers and instrumentally virtuous. Motown's publicity machine relished the comparison, doing nothing to discourage popular rumours that they were uncle and nephew."[23]

Motown's desire to establish Charles—at the height of his popularity at the time of Wonder's first recordings—as the primary reference point for Wonder was made explicit in Wonder's first, unreleased album, *A Tribute to Uncle Ray,* which, according to Michael Lydon, displays Wonder's "eleven-year-old voice piping Ray's barrel-chested originals."[24] Less explicitly, the trumpeting of Wonder as a genius in *Little Stevie Wonder: The 12 Year Old Genius* (1963), his first released album, further strengthened this tie to Charles, whose "genius" albums had already begun to fundamentally link Charles's image to that term. Leon E. Wynter writes that, for white adolescents in the early sixties, "Stevie Wonder was just the blind kid who sang a number in one of the beach-blanket movies, a novelty act. To black kids, the name Stevie Wonder was always mentioned with 'genius,' the only one of their own widely regarded as such."[25]

The apparent obviousness of the connection between Ray Charles and Stevie Wonder may explain why, over the course of the four decades in which they shared the spotlight, the two blind superstars maintained a certain distance from each other, at least professionally. Although Wonder and Charles never recorded together, Wonder has said, "We talked about it. There's a song I wrote, and I was hoping we would be able to do it. It's called "You're Too Much for My Eyes to See, I've Got to Touch You.' It's really a nice song. Timewise, though, we just couldn't work it out."[26] One suspects, however, that more than the logistics of clearing schedules was responsible for the failure of this collaboration to take place. After his first successes, Ray Charles did not remain significantly productive as a songwriter, and over the years it was his ability to choose appropriate material and collaborators that sustained his career. Given this sensitivity, Charles's resistance to referencing his blindness in the service of a song that would certainly strike many listeners as, at best, a novelty piece and, at worst, a very bad joke is not hard to fathom.

On the other hand, Wonder's willingness to not only write such a song but to consider recording it with another blind artist may reflect the fact that his ability to generate his own material gave him much more daring and "play" in the fashioning of his public image than the more conservative Charles. Reflecting the majority position, Gail Mitchell describes the five 1970s albums that ground Wonder's reputation—*Music of My Mind* (1972), *Talking Book* (1972), *Innervisions* (1973), *Fulfillingness' First Finale* (1974) and *Songs in the Key of Life* (1976)—as "cohesive, complex rhythmic treatises on love, life and racial and social issues."[27] Still, although Wonder's career has garnered him an Academy Award for best song, twenty-two (at last count) Grammy awards, and membership in both the Rock and Roll Hall of Fame and the Songwriters Hall of Fame, his work has sometimes been accused of being less than thoroughly convincing emotionally. According to Timothy White, "[Wonder's] signature songs are a voracious accumulation of contemporary leitmotifs, wedded to addled but affecting lyrics that are transporting when experienced, but embarrassing when written out."[28] White argues that "aptly— too aptly—there is scant emotion in his work save wonderment, few instincts beyond a sublime disavowal, no outlook firmer than anticipation—the blind bedazzling the blind."[29]

Although it's doubtful that many of those who have actually followed Wonder's career closely would find their admiration for Wonder's work shaken by White's critique, in terms of information value, a phrase like "the blind bedazzling the blind" is both literally meaningless and revelatory as a critical engagement with the work of a blind songwriter. It indicates the way in which Wonder's condition and the metaphorization of blindness in general might provide a reference point for attempts to question the legitimacy of his worldview. Such accusations imply, in usually covert but consistent ways, that Wonder's "vision" of the world is limited because he has no "real" vision of it. For instance, according to James Haskins and Kathleen Benson, "The words to many of his songs reveal a surprising lack of understanding of the politics of the black American experience, not to mention the American experience in general."[30]

Alternatively, reflecting another standard way of "reading" blind people, other critics have used Wonder's sightlessness to position him as someone who is especially farseeing. One of the songs that has often been read as evidence of Wonder's status as a visionary is, not surprisingly, "Visions," of which Wonder once said, "I hope it will be the song I'm remembered for."[31] In explaining the "inner visions" that he believes compensate for his lack of "outer vision," Wonder has remarked: "In a way I have to use my imagination to go places, to write words about things that I have heard people talk about. But in my music and in being blind I'm able to associate what people say with what's inside of me."[32] For instance, in this song Wonder writes:

> People hand in hand
> Have I lived to see the milk and honey land?
> Where hate's a dream and love forever stands
> Or is this a vision in my mind?

It is both his knowledge of the world as seeable and his faith in the possibility that it might be transcendable that Wonder establishes over the course of this song.

It is not through linguistic happenstance that Wonder positions a "milk and honey land" as the site of this transcendence. Throughout his recording career, he has repeatedly acknowledged and referenced his Christian faith and made it clear that he considers his manifestly secular music to be firmly in the service of that faith. In a 2004 interview, Wonder said: "I'm only being used as a vehicle through which comes encouragement, inspiration, hope and some clarity. The blessings of these songs that I receive from God come through me, to be heard and felt. It is an honor to do it, and I never forget the honor."[33] Such statements place Wonder solidly within the framework that generations of blind artists have used to distance themselves from the notion that they harbor resentment or anger about their condition.[34] When placed in their generative contexts, the seemingly "unrealistic" statements that blind celebrities like Helen Keller, Fanny Crosby, Ray Charles, and Wonder often made about the possibility of peaceful coexistence among different groups are rarely as naive as clear-eyed "realists" often make them out to be.

Like Rahsaan Roland Kirk, whose genre-busting eclecticism influenced him, Stevie Wonder, as a songwriter, performer, and public figure, has consistently referenced his blindness as a significant but not primary component of his sense of himself in the world. For instance, his album *Talking Book* features a cover photograph of Wonder without the dark glasses that by then had become standard equipment for blind performers. This choice forces the viewer to look at or at least reflect upon Wonder's eyes. Additionally, the words "talking book" hold a particular meaning for blind people, and the album features the title in Braille alongside the regular print. Understandably, Wonder was quite upset when he discovered that the original British version of the album featured a mis-Brailling of the title as "picture book," a phrase that nullified the very inclusiveness that the original title had been designed to evoke. The title *Talking Book* also indicates Wonder's perhaps unconscious, but still interesting signifying engagement of his blindness with his African heritage by way of the image of the talking book, which Henry Louis Gates Jr. would later establish as one of the premier tropes of African American culture's movement from orality to literacy.[35]

Stevie Wonder's well-known good nature concerning his blindness may explain the frequency with which his condition and, especially, his "blindisms" have been parodied or made the subject of jokes by comedians and why such ribbing has generated relatively little adverse critical comment from activists for the disabled. The most notable of these comic performances were those of Eddie Murphy during his stint on the show *Saturday Night Live*. Although rapturously received by the show's "hip" audiences, as Frank Sanello reported in a passage that is almost as offensive as Murphy's routine itself, Murphy's "grotesque impression of Stevie Wonder's Tourette-like tics offended handicapped people of all colors."[36] Although there is in fact nothing necessarily "Tourette-like" about Wonder's mannerisms, the most notable of his blindisms, and the one that grounded Murphy's impersonation, is the swaying motion— "shoulders back, face lifted, head bobbing side to side as he sings"—that has become an immediately recognizable component of Wonder's stage presence.[37] In their authorized but controversial biography of Wonder's mother, Lula Hardaway, Dennis Love and Stacy Brown report that early in Wonder's life, "everyone had tried to get Stevie to concentrate on stopping that odd mannerism, but he said he couldn't—he didn't even realize he was doing it."[38] In fact, this mannerism hampered Motown's efforts to fully "normalize" the young performer in relation to the media culture of the 1960s: "In the early years of Stevie's career, Motown had great difficulty in booking any television work for Stevie at all in America. . . . Television producers thought that the way Stevie jerked his head around might upset viewers."[39] Ironically, because of Murphy's sketches and Wonder's increasing familiarity to American audiences as African Americans became more common presences on network television in the 1970s and 1980s, it was television that solidified this gesture as an indicative marker of the singer's persona.

Reflecting the degree to which Eddie Murphy's impersonation became associated with the singer, and Wonder's increasing recognition as an iconic figure in American musical and cultural history, at one point Murphy considered starring in a film biography based on Wonder's life. However serious it may have been, the comedian's desire to extend the range of his professional engagement with Wonder's image apparently turned out to be a very different proposition from the sketches in which he had offered a more fitful enactment of Wonder's "difference." The failure of the Wonder biopic to come to fruition may reflect Murphy's and his consultants' realization of the potential for embarrassment and critical backlash that a feature-length extension of Murphy's controversial impersonation of the singer might have caused. The project's failure may also have been influenced by the growing power of the disability rights community to bring negative attention to such cavalier disregard of their sensibilities and concerns as Murphy's performances seemed to reveal.

Recently, in the wake of the critical and commercial success of the Ray Charles biopic *Ray,* Wonder, when asked about the prospect of a film about his life, responded:

I plan to do a book, and I'm excited about the prospects of a film. . . . It would be very inspirational in the things that I went through growing up as a little boy being blind and the things my mother had to contend with plus my brothers and sister in the days before Little Stevie Wonder and Stevie Wonder. Then maybe there would be another film about the second half of my life. We're still telling that story now.[40]

It is not surprising that Wonder is open to the idea of a film about his life, but it is interesting that he imagines it as being "inspirational," rather than the kind of normalizing tell-all that the film *Ray* was apparently intended to be. This indicates the degree to which for many, apparently even Wonder himself, Wonder can be read as what has disparagingly and—given what it takes to actually become one—unfairly been called a supercrip. Barbara Hillyer describes "supercrips" as "individuals who succeed brilliantly beyond what seem to be immovable barriers to their 'normal' functioning."[41] In other words, supercrips both exemplify and transcend their condition. Of the untold number of letters that Wonder receives, it has been reported that "the most touching letters and tapes were those in which other handicapped people told Stevie about things that they had done. But, they said, if Stevie had not encouraged them with his determination, they would not even have tried."[42] Beyond its usefulness as a means of grounding the cinematic recounting of his life, Wonder's awareness of his status as an "inspiration" to other disabled people is reflected in the yeoman service he has provided in donations and benefit concerts for organizations committed to improving conditions for the disabled.[43]

Over the years, however, Wonder's consciousness-raising efforts have been hampered by the difficulty that even the most articulate disabled people have in conveying to the unimpaired the inevitable social challenges engendered by their conditions in ways that don't position them as victims or objects of pity. Although album titles like *Talking Book* and *Innervisions* obviously reference his inability to see, Wonder's utilization of his own experience of blindness in the service of consciousness-raising was strikingly enacted in the publicity stunt—what he called the "sensual preview"—that he orchestrated for the release of *Innervisions*. Haskins and Benson relate the incident:

The flagship song on *Innervisions* was "Living for the City," and to introduce the album to the press, Stevie invited a group of journalists to go on a bus tour of New York City. When they were ready to board the bus, they found that they were to wear blindfolds for the trip, so that they could hear the city, experience it in the way that Stevie himself did. . . .

After they had ridden around town blindfolded for nearly an hour, to give them a sense of the physical reality of Stevie's world, they were taken to the studio to hear *Innervisions* for the first time.[44]

Despite the provocativeness of such gestures, it has consistently been proven that such simulation or consciousness-raising does not effectively reveal the issues that the disabled face when dealing with a world that does not adequately accommodate their impairment. Entering into the experience of disability by way of simulation is often experienced by the able-bodied as a form of discomfort followed by a counterproductive tension-relieving return to "normality."[45]

According to Robert A. Scott, "It is no accident that the blind persons who become most completely integrated into the larger society possess wealth, fame, or exceptional talent. These people can exchange prestige or money for the favors they must accept in order to function in daily life."[46] With this in mind, many aspects of Stevie Wonder's life and career take on a different light when they are compared to those of his friend and erstwhile collaborator Lee Garrett. Seven years older than Wonder and born blind, Garrett cowrote such classic Wonder songs as "Signed, Sealed, Delivered I'm Yours" and "It's A Shame." However, after a promising start in which he became the first black artist signed to Chrysalis Records, Garrett soon experienced the ups and downs that an impaired artist who lacked the backing of a paternalistically invested company like Motown could expect.[47] Although he achieved some success as a songwriter and radio personality, Garrett—like Paul Pena, far away from the limelight that has shone on Wonder—had to struggle with the typical problems that blind people face in a world that does not make particular provisions for those who are both poor and disabled.

These problems were made tragically clear in 1977 when Stevie Wonder's four-hour-long effort to talk a despondent Garrett out of committing suicide made its way into the press. As Garrett later recounted this incident, during which he had locked himself in a bathroom with a gun, "Business and personal problems had built up over the last few months and in the beginning of July seemed so overwhelming that I didn't see any way out of them."[48] Reflecting on the differences between the lives of most blind people and Wonder's life—Wonder, upon his twenty-first birthday, was given one million dollars in Motown royalties that had accrued in the federally managed trust fund that had been in place during his minority—Garrett has said:

> From when he was thirteen he never actually had to find out things about life. Like where to—physically—go. People would walk him. They would do anything for him. He never had to hit his head against a wall because other people would see to it that he didn't. He never had a chance to do things in private, find out things about himself. There were always people around him. Always. When he dropped something there was always someone to pick it up. And if Stevie picked it up himself he did it for fun, for the kick of it. But he never had to.[49]

The differences in their circumstances became even more apparent in 1985 when Garrett accused Wonder of appropriating his song "I Just Called to Say I Love You" and sued him for ten million dollars. Garrett later dropped the lawsuit when it was revealed that, beyond their shared titles, there were no significant musical similarities between the writers' two songs.[50]

The fact that Wonder's friendship with Garrett survived such an unpleasant episode is not as surprising as it might initially seem. As his years of activism reveal, Stevie Wonder, without doubt, has always been keenly aware of the frustrations and general lack of opportunities that most blind people face even today and of the distance between his life and theirs. Throughout his life and especially since his majority, Wonder has benefited from what could, somewhat fancifully, be called the cyborgean prosthetics of privilege. Wonder's virtually unlimited access to cutting-edge technology has allowed him to imagine and pursue possibilities well beyond those of the average impaired person.[51] Wonder himself has made the same point more straightforwardly: "Quite naturally with the technical advancements that are being made there are a great many things you can do."[52]

In the specific context of his musical career, Wonder was fortunate that the moment at which he achieved the independence that enabled him to do his own thing as an artist was also the moment at which the sonic prosthesis par excellence, the synthesizer, began to fully reveal its revolutionary potential as a "musical" instrument, not just as a technological novelty. When the adult Wonder's blindness could no longer be placed under the sign of "cuteness," it was the synthesizer that made it possible for him to reinvent himself as a prosthetically enhanced and up-to-date cyborgean soulman. James F. Perone observes, "It was Stevie Wonder who, perhaps more than anyone else, made electronic synthesizers an integral part of popular music in the 1970s."[53] In the public eye, Wonder went from being a boy to being something more than just a man. In the early 1970s, by way of the widespread dissemination of pictures of the now maturely handsome young man in front of his banks of machines, he became, for many, the image of the synthetically enhanced and therefore superhuman and supermodern music maker, more of a visionary than even his most committed fans could have expected him to become. It was impossible to feel sorry for or superior to someone who once again seemed to have the world at his "fingertips."

Over the last three decades, the relationship between Stevie Wonder and the implicitly utopian possibilities of advanced technology have grown even stronger. For instance, Wonder decisively reinforced his position as a pacesetter for exploring the potentially transformative relationship between disability and technology by establishing the SAP/Stevie Wonder Vision Awards, "which are given for products, people, and organizations that aid the blind and visually impaired."[54] Although in reality the benefits that technology has offered the disabled have usually been as a means of providing them with increased functionality as people with disabilities, rather than as a means for "solving" their condition, technology's public dialogue with disability is almost always either explicitly or covertly powered by the notion of cure.

Like Christopher Reeve, during his problematic years as a figurehead for disability activism, Wonder has also had to accept the reality of a public consciousness that believes—despite his achievement of a level of success that places him in the highest strata of creative accomplishment—that his situation would somehow simply be "better" if he could just see. For example, "in November 1999, Stevie stunned a congregation in a Detroit church by announcing that he was undergoing tests to determine whether or not he would be a candidate to receive a retinal implant that could give him some vision."[55] Surely, despite the newsworthiness of a sighted Wonder, from the start it must have been either known or strongly suspected that the nature of the singer's blindness made him an inappropriate candidate for the procedure. In any case, it is still highly experimental and unproven, even for those blind from retinitis pigmentosa, the type of blindness most likely to be aided by the procedure in the event that it is ever perfected. Stevie Wonder is probably the most famous blind person in the world, and a seeing Stevie Wonder is virtually unthinkable. It is his status as a "visionless visionary," "a sightless font of insight," that, for better or worse, has defined Wonder's public image since the early 1980s, when it became more difficult to laud him simply as a consistent hitmaker with his finger seemingly glued to the pulse of the pop music forefront.

To a great extent, Wonder's failure to make the transition to the music video age, and the subsequent decline in his production of hit singles, may reflect the fact that, despite the high production values of many of his clips, there is something essentially unnerving about watching a performer in a video that, one knows, he himself has never seen. This disconnect served to undermine the image of creative self-determination that had been central to Wonder's persona. I argued earlier that blind "classic" blues singers would have been alien to the glamorizing ethos of 1920s blues culture. Similarly, as a blind man, Wonder became just as great a misfit in the image-oriented world of early MTV and BET. In his video "So What the Fuss," Wonder attempted to circumvent this situation by offering the first video to deploy image description.

Recently, as an effect of the deaths of such legendary performers as Marvin Gaye, Curtis Mayfield, Rick James, Luther Vandross, and most significantly Ray Charles, Stevie Wonder has taken on even greater iconic status for the neo-soul artists who have emerged in the wake of the diversification of hip-hop beyond the cultural and expressive parameters of its early years. Although Wonder was initially marginalized by the ocularcentric forces that transformed the world of popular music in the early 1980s, both he and his music have increasingly been recontextualized and validated by an emerging cadre of self-consciously "aware" black artists for whom Wonder's professional longevity holds a utopian appeal in a musical culture in which the shelf life of even the most acclaimed performers has become distressingly brief. The quest of younger black artists like India Arie, Alicia Keys, and John Legend for cultural legitimation and a sense of continuity with the rest of the African American aesthetic and expressive tradition has been sparked by the extension of hip-hop beyond its provenance as the look and sound of 1980s African American youth culture. Although hip-hop is increasingly recognized as a performative site that spans the entire range of black popular culture, it is, tellingly, the only form of black popular music that has failed to sustain the career of a single blind or disabled performer. This absence makes it clear that, unlike those that preceded it, this space does not span the entire range of African American people. The failure of Wonder's extravagantly gifted protégé Raul Midón to achieve any significant commercial success is especially telling. Despite the usually regrettable forces that caused the impairments of blind performers, it is with both regret and a compensating sense of rightness that we must face the fact that the narrative of blind performers as significant forces in African American music will and probably should end as it began, with Wonder.

Notes

INTRODUCTION

1. I use the term "blind and visually impaired" in this instance to make clear my awareness that there are many degrees of vision loss that fall into the category of legal blindness. In order to avoid the ungainliness of repeating the phrase "blind and visually impaired" ad nauseam throughout the book, I will use the general term "blind people" to refer to the artists whose lives and work I will be discussing and to blind people as a group. Although some of these performers—most notably, for instance, Art Tatum and Sonny Terry—may have had significant levels of residual vision, they all lived with degrees of vision loss that constitute legal blindness and experienced the issues that affect blind people.

2. Michalko, *Difference That Disability Makes.*

3. Cruz, *Culture on the Margins.* Cruz asks: "What if we were to follow the particular musical practice, object, artifact, or symbol—or an ensemble of such practices and "things"—through certain aspects of its social circulation over time? Which social cells and cultural forms would music illuminate? Which individuals, groups, economic classes, or institutions would we encounter? Which relations of power would come into view? Which ideological configurations would be important? Which among the range of developments would be more prevalent?" (8).

4. As Donald Schon has written, "Blindness research looks rather like a cross-section of what you would see if sociologists, engineers, persons concerned with sensory awareness, and the like, were to pursue their discipline-oriented interests in ways that happen to intersect around the subject of blindness" ("Research on the Blindness System[s]," 104).

5. For a comprehensive consideration of the changing perceptions of people with disabilities from the Middle Ages through the nineteenth century, see Covey, *Social Perceptions.*

6. Koestler, *Unseen Minority,* 411.

7. Kuppers, *Disability and Contemporary Performance,* 31.

8. Quoted in Koestler, *Unseen Minority,* 184.

9. Stiker, *History of Disability,* 14.

10. Yuan, "Celebrity Freak," 378.

11. R. Scott, *Making of Blind Men,* 3.

12. R. Scott, *Making of Blind Men,* 14.

13. Koestler, *Unseen Minority,* 45.

14. Rusalem, *Coping with the Unseen Environment,* 6.

15. Rusalem, *Coping with the Unseen Environment,* 7. The ethnic variability of disability is still reflected, e.g., in the fact that even now, as Cabbil and Gold report, "African Americans are twice as likely to be visually impaired as are whites of comparable social status" ("African Americans with Visual Impairments," 59).

16. Today "nine out of 10 of the world's blind people live in developing countries, with nearly 60 percent of all the blind people in the world living in sub-Saharan Africa, China, and India. The World Health Organization estimates that up to 80 percent of global blindness is preventable through nutritional, therapeutic, and sanitation-improvement programs" (Shelly et al., *Encyclopedia of Blindness,* 28).

17. As the philosopher Kelly Oliver has suggested, "To see and be seen are not just the results of mechanical and photic energies, but also of social energies" (*Witnessing,* 14).

18. Hollins, *Understanding Blindness,* 10.

19. Berthold Lowenfeld reports, "It is generally agreed that individuals who lose their sight before about five years of age do not retain any useful visual imagery" (*Berthold Lowenfeld on Blindness and Blind People,* 67).

20. Goode, *World without Words,* 223.

21. D. Marks, *Disability,* 104.

22. R. French, *From Homer to Helen Keller,* 3.

23. Safford and Safford, *History of Childhood and Disability,* 143.

24. Corker, *Deaf and Disabled,* 5–6.

25. To a great extent, the existence of a sense of communal identity among the deaf has been stabilized linguistically by the d/Deaf distinction that characterizes much writing on deafness. Owen Wrigley writes: "The use of the term Deaf, in uppercase, is now widely used to refer to the cultural category of self-identification. The lowercase term refers to the simple fact of audiological impairment and is distinct from the process of self-identity" (*Politics of Deafness,* 14).

26. S. French and Swain, *From a Different Viewpoint,* 10.

27. Berthold Lowenfeld notes that "one cannot avoid talking about 'the blind' as one cannot avoid such other generalizations as 'the French.' . . . Intragroup differences are generally taken for granted and do not need to be repetitiously stressed nor do they become more accentuated or plausible by changing terms, such as substituting 'blind persons' for 'the blind" (*Changing Status of the Blind,* vii–viii).

28. Reprinted by permission of the author.

29. According to Barnes, Mercer, and Shakespeare, "disability art entails using art to expose the discrimination and prejudice disabled people face and to generate group consciousness and solidarity" (*Exploring Disability,* 206).

30. Kirtley, *Psychology of Blindness,* 99.

31. Chevigny and Braverman, *Adjustment of the Blind,* 92.

32. R. French, *From Homer to Helen Keller,* 204.

33. Csikszentmihalyi, "Creativity and Genius," 42.

34. Simi Linton points out, "Ableism also includes the idea that a person's abilities or characteristics are determined by disability" (*Claiming Disability,* 9).

35. For a general consideration of this issue, see Boulter, "Living with Blindness," 166.

36. Boulter, "Living with Blindness," 113.

37. Safford and Safford, *History of Childhood and Disability*, 123.

38. Donald D. Kirtley observes, "Though many blind people deny any aware-ness of darkness claiming instead a visual neutrality that is neither dark nor light, the fact remains that most people associate visual loss with darkness" (*Psychology of Blindness*, 84).

CHAPTER I

1. Bogdan, *Freak Show*, 2.

2. In fact, much of nineteenth-century popular culture was characterized by what Iris Marion Young calls "the objectification and overt domination of despised bodies" (*Justice and the Politics of Difference*, 124).

3. Reiss, *Showman and the Slave*, 101.

4. Grob, *Deadly Truth*, 219.

5. R. Adams, *Sideshow U.S.A.*, 165. For comparative evidence of the range of responses to Tom's life and career as reflected in *Dwight's Journal of Music*, the most influential musical publication in nineteenth-century America, see Riis, "Culti-vated White Tradition," 156–76.

6. Paul Edwards and James Walvin observe: "White freaks were always exhib-ited as oddities, whose value lay in the way they were distinguished from the rest of their species. Black people, on the other hand, were exhibited as typical of their race" (quoted in Abrahams, "Images of Sara Bartman," 225).

7. Frost, *Never One Nation*, 4–5.

8. In the nineteenth century, the term "idiot" was used to refer to those indi-viduals who in modern terminology are considered "profoundly" retarded, or with an IQ of less than 25. "Morons" were those with IQs of 55 to 70, and "imbeciles" had IQs of 25 to 55. For a detailed consideration of the evolution of this terminol-ogy and its affects in determining the life chances of those with mental disabilities, see Noll, *Feeble-Minded in Our Midst*.

9. In his study of the phenomenon, Michael J. A. Howe writes that "'idiot sa-vant' is the term that has most frequently been used to designate mentally handi-capped individuals who are capable of outstanding achievements at particular tasks" (*Fragments of Genius*, 5). When discussing the historically specific deployment of this concept, I will use the term "idiot savant." Generally, however, I will use the more appropriate and certainly now less disturbing term "mentally impaired sa-vant."

10. Blind Tom Bethune was in many ways a classic savant, given that, according to Leon K. Miller, "most musical savants are male, visually impaired, and have a his-tory of language disorder" (*Musical Savants*, 190).

11. For a fascinating account of the issues that arise when dealing with Blind Tom in a disability studies context, see Krentz, "'Vacant Receptacle'?"

12. Barbara Schmidt points out: "Although Tom's parents were married, the prevailing custom of the time dictated that female slaves and their children retain the names of their owners. Following slavery tradition, Tom received the name Thomas Greene Bethune" (*Archangels Unaware*).

13. Blindness and other eye ailments were relatively common conditions

among blacks on Southern plantations. Much of this blindness could be traced to the nutritional inadequacies of the slaves' diets and deficient and misguided health care. Today the consequences of such deficiencies are reflected in the fact that blindness is still, when compared to the countries of the West, a disproportionately common condition in the world's poorer nations.

14. Sanjek, *American Popular Music,* 2: 215.

15. Plantinga, "Piano and the Nineteenth Century," 3.

16. Although he would become the most discussed and seen blind American musical performer of his time, Blind Tom was not the first blind musician to achieve success on the concert stages of America and Europe. The most significant of these artists was the pianist Maria Theresia von Paradis (1759–1824). In many ways, von Paradis's life and career offer an almost perfectly inverted image of Tom's. Herbert C. Covey writes: "She traveled throughout the world demonstrating her talent. Her success demonstrated that people with blindness were capable of major accomplishments. She was inspirational to others and helped educators . . . build public support for their schools" (*Social Perceptions,* 170). For a brief account of von Paradis's life and career, see Lowenfeld, *Changing Status of the Blind,* 61–62.

17. Quoted in Southall, *Blind Tom: The Post–Civil War Enslavement,* 27. When considering the extent to which Tom was subjected to the nineteenth-century discourses of "enfreakment," it is important to remember that music was not the only "marvelous" component of his performances: "He also could recite speeches in foreign languages and mimic the cadences and inflections of well-known political figures" (Bunch, "Strange Harmonies," 18).

18. R. Davis, "Blind Tom," 107. For more on the racial politics of Davis's article, see Sizer, *Political Work of Northern Women Writers,* 153.

19. Quoted in Jay, *Learned Pigs,* 319.

20. F. O. Jones,"Blind Tom," 15.

21. For an example of the difficulties that this project entailed, see the almost comically incoherent image of Tom as both a refined gentleman and a "weak-minded Negro" provided in John A'Becket's "Blind Tom as He Is Today," which was originally printed at the Lercheses' instigation in the *Ladies' Home Journal* on 15 Sept. 1898.

22. Despite their efforts, the link between Tom and the discourses of slavery was seemingly unbreakable. In Feb. 1894, in a motion brought against Stutzbach Bethune Lerche for the unpaid balance to the lawyer who had represented her in her case against the Bethune family, that lawyer, John McGrone, asserted: "In using the name of Blind Tom in the motion I am about to make, don't let it be thought that I am going to begin another fight for the freedom of that poor old man. Nothing, not even the emancipation proclamation, has ever freed him, and he is held in slavery as strong to-day as before the war" (Abbott and Seroff, *Out of Sight,* 335).

23. Rouse, "We Can Never Remain Silent," 129.

24. Hutton, *Early Black Press in America,* ix.

25. Thomson, "Narrative of Deviance and Delight," 100.

26. M. Holmes, *Fictions of Affliction,* 167. Before the racist reading of Tom had become standardized, Long Grabs, one of the first commentators on Tom's performances, wrote in the *Fayetteville Observer* for 19 May 1862, "This poor blind boy is cursed with but little of human nature; he seems to be an unconscious agent acting

as he is acted on, and his mind a vacant receptacle where Nature's [*sic*] stores her jewels to recall them at her pleasure" ("Untitled.").

27. Transcribed from *Marvelous Musical Prodigy*, 20. Geneva Southall, the dean of Blind Tom scholars, has argued that "such an amazing literary feat should have been in itself enough to raise questions about Tom's so-called imbecility." I believe, however, that although the poem does raise interesting questions, it doesn't significantly undermine notions of Tom's mental deficits. Despite the unsurpassable value of her career-long critical engagement with the Blind Tom phenomenon, Southall's work on Tom, in its generally de-disabling tenor, often fails to fully consider disability as a historically specific discursive phenomenon. Too often Southall's attempt to position Tom as a self-conscious black genius manfully trying to free himself from the web of American racism reflects the ways in which the reality of disability as a simultaneously individualizing and deindividualizing corporeal state can be obscured by explanatory narratives that mystify rather than specify the challenges with which a particular disabled person might have been grappling. Accordingly, I believe that in this instance, Southall's championing of Tom leads to a too-ready acceptance of what seems to be an obviously fraudulent document. Southall, *Post-Civil War*, 73.

28. Hull, *On Sight and Insight*, 51.

29. Perry and Roy, *Light in the Shadows*, 113.

30. Lowenfeld, *Our Blind Children*, 103.

31. I will more closely consider the issue of the impact of blindisms on the reception of blind performers in the chapter on Stevie Wonder.

32. Riis, "Blind Tom."

33. Riis, "Blind Tom."

34. Riis, "Blind Tom."

35. Ezra, *Colonial Unconscious*, 102.

36. The type of mass hysteria that Riis projects onto the Blind Tom phenomenon is more reasonable when considering the career and international reception of a vaguely racialized white performer like the hugely successful Louisiana Creole pianist Louis Moreau Gottschalk. S. Frederick Starr notes of Gottschalk that, like Elvis, he "epitomized aspects of an emerging American culture that some loved and others loathed." Ironically, perhaps because of the refusal of many "elite" American critics to accept the legitimacy of his talent as evidence of anything but successful marketing, it was Gottschalk who, in a letter in his posthumously published *Notes of a Pianist*, would offer one of the most stinging assessments of both the singularity and the extent of Tom's gifts. See Gottschalk, *Notes of a Pianist*, 95–96.

37. Henson,"Neurological Aspects of Musical Experience," 10.

38. Treffert, *Extraordinary People*, 19.

39. For general accounts of Boone's life, see Battersby, *Blind Boone;* Sears, "Boone, John William"; and Harrah, *Blind Boone.*

40. Fuell, *Blind Boone*, 70.

41. Quoted in Fuell, *Blind Boone*, 163.

42. Reed, *Holy Profane*, 24.

43. For an overview of the music associated with minstrel shows, see Winan, "Early Minstrel Show Music."

44. Jasen and Tichenor, *Rags and Ragtime*, 1.

45. Fuell, *Blind Boone,* 139.

46. It was this threat that some have, I believe too sweepingly, argued prevented black men from achieving the degree of success as blues singers that black women achieved during the 1920s.

47. For the most authoritative and comprehensive account of American minstrelsy, see Eric Lott's magisterial *Love and Theft.*

48. D. Scott, *Singing Bourgeois,* 82.

49. Waldo, *This Is Ragtime,* 18.

50. Quoted in Battersby, *Blind Boone,* 56.

51. Quoted in Fuell, *Blind Boone,* 153.

52. Cather, *My Ántonia,* 178.

53. Cather, *My Ántonia,* 183.

54. Schafer and Riedel, *Art of Ragtime,* 38–39.

55. For accounts of the lives and careers of the McKoy Sisters and William Henry Johnson, see Martell, *Millie-Christine;* Cook,"Of Men, Missing Links, and Nondescripts"; Bogdan, *Freak Show,* 134–42; and B. Adams, *E Pluribus Barnum,* 157–64.

56. Bullock, *Afro-American Periodical Press,* 196.

57. Harrah, *Blind Boone,* 100.

58. Quoted in Battersby, *Blind Boone,* 24.

CHAPTER 2

1. Barry Hansen points out that "the word 'blind' was commonly tacked on to the name of any sightless entertainer in the 1920s" (*Rhino's Cruise through the Blues,* 47).

2. Petra Kuppers writes, "When the disabled, 'extraordinary,' or other body is the freak, it cannot at the same time be a focus for communality" (*Disability and Contemporary Performance,* 45).

3. The performers whose lives and music ground my work in this chapter are Blind Lemon Jefferson (1893–1929), Blind Blake (early 1890s–ca. 1933), Blind Boy Fuller/Fulton Allen (1907–41), Blind Willie McTell (1901–59), Sleepy John Estes (1904–77), and Sonny Terry/Saunders Terry (1911–86).

4. Witek. "Blindness as a Rhetorical Trope," 192.

5. Witek, "Blindness as a Rhetorical Trope," 193.

6. The image from which the more enterprising blind bluesmen sought to distance themselves was given one of its earliest representations in William Faulkner's *Flags in the Dust,* published in 1927: "Against the wall squatting a blind negro beggar with a guitar and a wire frame holding a mouth organ to his lips, patterned the background of smells and sounds with a plaintive reiteration of rich monotonous chords, rhythmic as a mathematical formula but without music. He was a man of at least forty years and his was the patient resignation of many sightless years" (quoted in Tosches, *Where Dead Voices Gather,* 236–37).

7. Reed, *Holy Profane,* 155–56.

8. Smart, *Disability, Society, and the Individual,* 86.

9. Covey, *Social Perceptions,* 39.

10. Ironically, the racial realities of American life in the 1920s and 1930s might actually have enhanced the freedom and social mobility of some blind black performers and their lead boys. In their wanderings along the back roads of the Jim Crow South, blind men had no fear of being dragooned into the forced labor to which sighted black men were often subjected during this period. Also, blind musicians benefited from many railroads' practice of letting blind people travel on trains for free or at half-price. For instance, "Congress in 1927 passed an amendment to the Interstate Commerce Act allowing common carriers to let any totally blind person accompanied by a guide be charged only one fare" (Lowenfeld, *Changing Status of the Blind,* 215). Of course, like all privileges in the South, these were not made as consistently available to blind blacks as they were to their white counterparts.

11. Mystification of the mobility of blind people has also been increased by the reluctance of many blind people, mindful of the sense of primitivism that it can evoke, to admit how great a role the sense of smell plays in their efforts to orient themselves and map their environment.

12. Trevor-Roper, *World through Blunted Sight,* 163.

13. Barlow, *Looking Up at Down,* 95.

14. R. French, *From Homer to Helen Keller,* 11.

15. Koestler, *Unseen Minority,* 109.

16. Michalko, *Difference that Disability Makes,* 151. According to Michalko, in such instances of "verbal passing," blind people "are showing themselves and sighted others that they (blind people) 'know' the sighted character of the world and, despite not being able to see it, 'know' that the world is seeable" (*Difference that Disability Makes,* 27).

17. After a review of the scholarly evidence, Harry McGurk concludes that at most "blindness is associated with delayed rather than deviant communicative development" ("Effectance Motivation," 110).

18. Transcribed in Titon, *Early Downhome Blues,* 27.

19. Transcribed in Titon, *Early Downhome Blues,* 115.

20. Quoted in McGurk, "Effectance Motivation," 110.

21. Tuttle and Tuttle, *Self-Esteem and Adjusting with Blindness,* 49.

22. Quoted in Kirtley, *Psychology of Blindness,* 44.

23. Monge, "Language of Blind Lemon Jefferson," 38.

24. Monge, "Language of Blind Lemon Jefferson," 47.

25. Berthold Lowenfeld states that "these substitutive color ideas exist not only as components of the blind person's world of imagery, but also as part of his vocabulary need to communicate with the world in common terms" (*Berthold Lowenfeld on Blindness and Blind People,* 71).

26. Kirtley, *Psychology of Blindness,* 43. In a passage that further reveals the potentially alienating effect of Monge's position, John M. Hull suggests that "when the sighted person draws attention to a little oddity in the use of a visual metaphor by a blind person, beneath this lies a subtle shift in the whole character of communication between sighted and blind people" (*On Sight and Insight,* 26).

27. Monge, "Language of Blind Lemon Jefferson," 65. In an essay that simply reproduces Monge's conclusions while extending notions of sensory compensation and of a relationship between blindness and duplicity, Christopher John Farley

asks, "Did Blind Lemon Jefferson have a special talent for the blues not in spite of but *because* of his visual impairment"? and "Was Jefferson's blindness part of his act? Perhaps imagining vision in song was his way of compensating for what he lacked in reality?" ("Visionary Blindness," 166, 170; emphasis in original). Chevigny and Braverman classically describe the ableist perspective that this statement reflects: "The blind man, it is held, cannot escape the melancholy imposed by his condition. He cannot really adjust to it. At best, he can only forget it for a while. If he denies that he experiences anything of the kind, he is not believed; instead, he is considered to be extremely courageous and brave about his situation" (*Adjustment of the Blind,* 146).

28. Transcribed in Levine, *Black Culture and Black Consciousness,* 251.

29. Transcribed in Sackheim, *Blues Line,* 346.

30. What Robert Garland writes of the ancient Graeco-Roman world seems to have been equally true for blacks in the rural American South: "Since only the well-to-do had the means to consult a physician, even a minor trauma, such as a broken arm or leg, fractured kneecap, or dislocated shoulder, was likely to result in permanent disability" (*Eye of the Beholder,* 210).

31. Transcribed in P. Oliver, *Story of the Blues,* 21.

32. Transcribed in Barlow, *Looking Up at Down,* 303.

33. Terminologically, when considering the range of blues recordings and artists, it is important to keep in mind Paul Oliver's useful caveat that "the crude classifications of country blues, city blues and classic blues . . . are so broad in their implications and so poorly distinguished as to be worthless for any practical purposes of analysis" (*Aspects of the Blues Tradition,* 13–14). In the context of this study, however, these categories continue to have a value as historical and stylistic place markers.

34. For the richest consideration of the sexual politics of the black women's blues tradition, see Angela Davis's classic text *Blues Legacies and Black Feminism.*

35. Kudlick, "Outlook of *The Problem,*" 206.

36. Kudlick, "Outlook of *The Problem,*" 200.

37. Limaye, "Sexuality and Women with Sensory Disabilities," 92.

38. The Center for Women's Policy Studies reports that even today "disabled women are raped and abused at a rate more than twice that of nondisabled women" (cited in L. Davis, *Bending Over Backwards,* 147).

39. Transcribed in Sackheim, *Blues Line,* 57.

40. Transcribed in Sackheim, *Blues Line,* 34.

41. Transcribed in Sackheim, *Blues Line,* 382.

42. Lowenfeld, *Berthold Lowenfeld on Blindness and Blind People,* 174.

43. Barasch, *Blindness,* 144.

44. Even as formidable a figure as the folk legend Leadbelly actively circulated and took great pride in the fact that for a number of years he had performed with Jefferson and served as his "eyes." Leadbelly memorialized this relationship in his songs "Blind Lemon Blues" and "My Friend Blind Lemon." For an account of this relationship, see Wolfe and Lornell, *Life and Legend of Leadbelly,* 42–48; Lornell, "Blind Lemon Meets Leadbelly."

45. Some of the best known of these artists were the duo "Mac and Bob" (Lester McFarland and Robert Gardner), who met while both were attending the

Kentucky Blind School; George Reneau ("The Blind Musician of the Smoky Mountains"); the Reverend Andrew Jenkins, an evangelist and songwriter better known as "Blind Andy"; the blind fiddler G. B. Grayson; Blind Jim Howard; Blind Ed Haley; Horton Barker; and the multi-instrumentalist Ernest Thompson. Other notables were the Grand Old Opry performers Blind Joe Mangrum and Schriver and Blind Bill Day (1860–1942) ("Jilson Setters"). Second in popularity to Riley Puckett among blind white country singers was Blind Alfred Reed. Even the great Doc Watson (1923–) never managed to achieve much commercial success beyond the folk circuit.

46. Burnett's "The Song of the Orphan Boy," an autobiographical account of how he lost his sight, is one of the most striking of the few such songs by blind songwriters. A singer who would later have a great influence on the folk revival movement is Emma Dusenberry, whom Ronald D. Cohen describes as "a blind singer living in Mena, Arkansas who was a repository of hundreds of songs and ballads" (*Rainbow Quest,* 45).

47. For an account of this relationship, see Wolfe, *Kentucky Country,* 21–22.

48. Lowe, *American Pop,* 113.

49. Lowe, *American Pop,* 113.

50. Milsap and Carter, *Almost like a Song,* 7.

51. Black, *War against the Weak,* 145.

52. Black, *War against the Weak,* 145.

53. Monbeck, *Meaning of Blindness,* 11.

54. Herrmann, *Helen Keller,* 177.

55. Farrell, *Story of Blindness,* 231.

56. For a particularly horrific example of this "blackening" of syphilis, see J. Jones, *Bad Blood.*

57. Beardsley, *History of Neglect,* 117. The disproportionate rates of blindness among blacks was also exacerbated by the fact that diseases like tuberculosis, which afflicted blacks in greater numbers than whites, and sickle-cell anemia, which in the United States is an almost exclusively black disease, can also cause blindness. For an overview of the most common historical causes of blindness, see Dobree, "Causes of Blindness."

58. For a comprehensive examination of the medicine show phenomenon, see McNamara, *Step Right Up.*

59. Quoted in Bastin, *Red River Blues,* n. 183.

60. Samuel K. Roberts writes: "Even after Emancipation, given the fact that medical schools in the nation refused to admit black would-be doctors, the national black community was medically underserved. The legacy of slavery in the form of economic tenuousness of black life translated into the pervasive inability of black families to pay for medical care, generally available through unsympathetic or paternalistic white doctors" (*African American Christian Ethics,* 239).

61. Reproduced in Bastin, *Red River Blues,* 215.

62. Chevigny and Braverman have parodically articulated the image of the blind beggar: "Toward the blind the world presents a face it turns to no other group on earth. Everyone else must struggle for his existence, must fight for his survival. The blind, however, need not want. Society, profoundly convinced of the utter helplessness of a man who has lost his sight, stands ever ready to help him, whether

his need be so small a thing as crossing the street or the larger one of food and shel-
ter for the rest of his days" (*Adjustment of the Blind,* 3). For a general consideration of
the social dynamics of begging and disability, see M. Holmes, *Fictions of Affliction.*

63. At one point Blind Boy Fuller, Gary Davis, and Sonny Terry played on the
streets of Durham, together constituting a virtual black blind supergroup. Because
the impetus for most blind country blues performers was such street singing, and
the guitar and harmonica were the instruments best suited for that profession, the
country blues tradition generated few blind pianists and, with only a handful of exceptions, very few pianists generally.

64. R. Scott, *Making of Blind Men,* 112. The relatively high number of impoverished African Americans who can currently be found begging on the subways and
sidewalks of most of this country's major cities may also reflect this dynamic.

65. Geremek, *Poverty,* 28.

66. Thomson, *Extraordinary Bodies,* 50.

67. Reproduced in Charters, *Sweet as the Showers of Rain,* 156.

68. Witek, "Blindness as a Rhetorical Trope," 189.

69. This notion is also reflected in the position of blind musicians in other cultures. For instance, in his study of Arabian music, Habib Hassan Touma reports
that in the nineteenth century, "the only persons allowed to perform at weddings in
front of women, besides female musicians, were blind musicians" (*Music of the
Arabs,* 13–14).

70. For a consideration of the performers and conditions that laid the groundwork for Jefferson's emergence, see D. Evans, "Musical Innovation."

71. Matt Backer humorously observes that "Blind Lemon Jefferson is perhaps
best known as the template for the joke which states that in order to be a blues man
one needs a handle that is comprised in equal parts of: an affliction, a fruit, and the
surname of a U.S. president" ("Guitar," 116).

72. For an informative but essentially anecdotal account of Jefferson's life and
career, see Uzzel, *Blind Lemon Jefferson.*

73. Alan B. Govenar and Jay F. Brakefield ask, concerning Jefferson, "Why
would a blind man wear glasses, as he does in one of the two known photographs of
him?" (*Deep Ellum and Central Track,* 62). The answer is that the glasses in this photograph were painted in so as to normalize Jefferson's closed eyed visage. In other
words, they serve the same normalizing function that dark glasses have come to
play in the official images of most blind public figures.

74. Santelli, *Big Book of Blues,* 241.

75. Quoted in Govenar, "That Black Snake Moan," 37. This eulogy reflects the
degree to which blindness has been a component of Christian culture and spiritual
and gospel music, a subject that I will explore in the following chapter.

76. Govenar, "Blind Lemon Jefferson," 14.

77. On various labels and documents, he is also listed as "Arthur (Blind) Blake,"
"Blind Arthur Blake," and "Arthur Blake".

78. Springer, *Authentic Blues,* 103.

79. Quoted in Charters, *Sweet as the Showers of Rain,* 144.

80. For instance, McTell inspired what is generally considered to be one of Bob
Dylan's greatest songs, the straightforwardly entitled classic "Blind Willie McTell."
Dylan also recorded pseudonymously under the name "Blind Boy Grunt."

81. Keil, *Urban Blues,* 34–35. In a direct rebuttal to Kiel, Bob Groom writes: "In *Urban Blues,* a generally well-reasoned and thought-provoking book, Charles Keil made a bitter and unjustified attack on the Folk Blues Festival audiences. He implied that most of the bluesmen who had appeared on it at the time of his writing had been old, infirm and musically incapable, a criticism very far from the truth. In reality, all of the performers who have taken part in the FBF [Folk Blues Festival] have been in full possession of their musical faculties, and there has been considerable variety in the composition of each festival, with no emphasis on any particular style or generation" (*Blues Revival,* 86–87).

82. Mark Priestly asserts that "impaired bodies cease to be 'out of place' or 'special' in old age when compared to other generational locations." Accordingly to Priestly, "It could be argued that the onset of impairment in later life reinforces the biographical identity of older people rather than disrupting it" ("Disability and Old Age," 86).

83. Groom, *Blues Revival,* 51. Consideration of Estes's life before his "comeback" reveals the destitution to which many country blues performers had been reduced after the collapse of the appeal for their music among African American audiences in the late 1940s. Samuel Charters described his first meeting with Estes: "Even knowing that he was in poor health, blind, and living in a poor shack, I still wasn't prepared for the sight of him, a gaunt, tall figure in dirty farm clothes, a shapeless straw hat on his head, sitting alone (*Sweet as the Showers of Rain,* 69–70).

84. Charters, *Country Blues,* 194.

85. Blind performers outside of the circuit of the blues proper include Blind Arvella Gray, Blind Pete, the accordionist Blind Jesse Harris, and the New Orleans street singer "Snooks" Eaglin.

In the context of the blues, Eaglin could be considered a "second-generation" blind bluesman. Eagan was born in 1936 and was therefore much younger than most of the other blind bluesmen, but his blindness no doubt contributed to the fact that, as Francis Davis writes, he was "among the very few younger black performers deemed 'authentic' by [1960s] white blues audiences" (*History of the Blues,* 215).

86. Ironically, Terry's sighted partner Brownie McGhee had begun his recording career by recording under the pseudonym "Blind Boy Fuller No. 2."

87. Also contributing to Terry's success until their legendary feuding led to the breakdown of the partnership in 1976 was the fact that he had in his partner Brownie McGhee the added benefit of a more or less constant "lead" man.

CHAPTER 3

1. Trevor-Roper, *World through Blunted Sight,* 160.

2. Herbert C. Covey points out that in the Bible, "no other disability received more attention than blindness" (*Social Perceptions,* 176).

3. Transcribed in Chenu, *Trouble I've Seen,* 235.

4. Barasch, *Blindness,* 55.

5. There were, of course, some spirituals that attempted to counter the idea that blind people and other disabled were passive figures somewhere outside of the rights of positive recognition and the obligations of communal responsibility. In

one song, we find the relatively self-assertive lines, "I may be blind an' cannot see / I'll meet you at the station / When the train comes along. / I may be lame an' cannot walk, / But I'll meet you at the station / When the train comes along."

6. Transcribed in Chenu, *Trouble I've Seen,* 278. Howard Thurman notes of this song that "the slave singers did a strange thing with this story. They identified themselves completely with the blind man at every point but the most critical one. In the song, the blind man does not receive his sight. The song opens with the cry; it goes through many nuances of yearning, but always it ends with the same cry with which it began" (Thurman, *Deep River,* 38).

7. Transcribed in Z. Holmes, "Encounter Jesus in Worship."

8. Transcribed in Cone, *Spirituals and the Blues,* 34.

9. Ruconich and Schneider, "Religions and Their Views of Blindness," 198.

10. Transcribed in Lornell, *"Happy in the Service of the Lord,"* 150.

11. Farrell, *Story of Blindness,* 4.

12. J. Smith and Carson, *Favorite Women Hymn Writers,* 84.

13. For accounts of Crosby's life and career, see Ruffin, *Fanny Crosby;* Loveland, *Blessed Assurance;* and Blumhofer, *Her Heart Can See.* For a general account of the role and impact of women in American hymnody, see Hobbs, "I Sing for I Cannot Be Silent." For evidence of the appeal of hymn writing for impaired and disabled white Christian women in the nineteenth and early twentieth centuries, see the brief biographies in J. Smith and Carson, *Favorite Women Hymn Writers.*

14. Quoted in Goff, *Close Harmony,* 27.

15. Edith Blumhofer suggests that "[Crosby's] texts voiced a popular understanding of evangelical Christianity that, there is reason to believe (from scattered newspaper accounts and later obituaries in the black press), rang true among many African Americans" (*Her Heart Can See,* 283). Upon her death, "the *Cleveland Journal,* a black newspaper, printed her photo with incidents from her life and the comment that her hymns were 'known and loved by nearly everyone'" (Blumhofer, *Her Heart Can See,* 329). The ecclesiastical range and transcultural force of Crosby's imagery are revealed by Jon Michael Spencer's assertion that "it is not at all surprising that, among the gospel hymnists, Fanny J. Crosby is best represented in *Yes Lord!* [the official hymnal of the Church of God in Christ] with fifteen hymns" (*Black Hymnody,* 154). In fact, it would be the Church of God in Christ that would most directly enable the careers of the most significant blind gospel singers.

16. Quoted in A. Young, *Woke Me Up This Morning,* 8 (ellipses in original).

17. Transcribed in George, "Lucie E. Campbell," 15.

18. Monge, "Blindness Blues," 112.

19. Monge, "Blindness Blues," 112.

20. Boyer, "Comparative Analysis of Traditional and Contemporary Gospel Music."

21. A similarly defamiliarizing effect was created by such celebrated recordings as Arizona Dranes's "Just Look," Reverend (Blind) Gary Davis's "I Saw the Light," and Blind Connie Williams's "I Can See Everybody's Mother, [but I] Can't See Mine." The last of these songs would become the first hit and one of the signature recordings of the best-known blind performers in the tradition of black gospel music, the Blind Boys of Alabama.

22. Goff, *Close Harmony,* 209.

23. Dupree and Dupree, *African-American Good News (Gospel) Music,* 89.

24. Wilds, *Raggin' the Blues,* 81. This reading of Johnson reflects the effort to remove blind blues and gospel singers from narratives of black modernity that would later come to fruition during the folk blues revival and would be so sharply excoriated by writers like Charles Keil and Barbara Dane. Johnson's supposedly singular degree of "authenticity" may also explain why his recording of "Dark Was the Night, Cold Was the Ground" was chosen for inclusion as an example of "earth culture" on the spacecraft *Voyager* (Humphrey, "Holy Blues," 126).

25. Humphrey, "Holy Blues," 125.

26. Lowe, *American Pop,* 96; Sante, "Blues Avant-Garde," 75. The violence to which Lowe refers reflects the most widely accepted account of Johnson's blinding, which reports that, after having been beaten by Johnson's father, the boy's stepmother threw a pan of water dosed with lye into the child's face as retaliation. Some have suggested that her target was actually Johnson's father and not Johnson himself. In either case, the assault left Johnson completely blind.

27. As early as 1933, Zora Neale Hurston wrote in her essay "Spirituals and Neo-Spirituals" that "as indefinite as hums sound, they also are formal and can be found unchanged all over the South" (17).

This tradition is in fact so long and well-known that the phrases "moaning the spirituals" and "moaning the blues" are veritable clichés in considerations of African American music. Michael W. Harris writes of the practice as it was incorporated into black church practices in the early twentieth century: "'Moaning' may be considered a set of performance practices, usually embellishments, that were applied to any of the genres of religious song that blacks then sang. . . . This ability to express oneself through the melody without singing the text made 'moaning' adaptable to widely varying circumstances" (*Rise of the Gospel Blues,* 22).

28. Hinson, *Fire in My Bones,* 42.

29. Quoted in Tilling, *"Oh, What A Beautiful City,"* 76.

30. Chevigny and Braverman, *Adjustment of the Blind,* 162.

31. Important among the lesser-known artists was the guitar-playing evangelist of the 1920s Blind Mamie Forehand, who usually sang with her husband, A. C. Forehand. The failure of the talented singer Blind Princess Stewart to achieve success in the world of gospel, despite the foundational role played by her predecessor Arizona Dranes in establishing the tradition and despite Stewart's association with Alex Bradford, one of the early titans of gospel, again indicates the reluctance of audiences across all musical genres to accept blind women as performers as readily as they have accepted blind men. The one exception has been the moderately successful jazz singer Diane Schuur.

32. Darden, *People Get Ready,* 145.

33. Bernice Johnson Reagon writes that "as a member of the COGIC church she [Dranes] worked as a religious musician within a denomination that was more open musically" (*If You Don't Go,* 23).

34. As for why so many of the blind gospel performers of the 1920s were affiliated with the Church of God in Christ, Horace Boyer observes that "this is perhaps no coincidence: the Pentecostal/Holiness church or Church placed heavy emphasis on healing and many of these singers were awaiting healing; the music was new and catchy; and donations were given with less pity and guilt when the blind person exhibited a talent" (*How Sweet the Sound,* 38).

35. The most popular gospel singing group recording for Paramount in the 1920s was the Norfolk Jubilee Quartet, led by the blind singer Norman "Crip" Harris. The blind pianists John W. Ephron and Blind Francis were also popular accompanists in the gospel world.

36. Although these groups were generally referred to as quartets, the number of members could vary considerably, with groups sometimes including as many as seven or eight members.

37. Lornell, *"Happy in the Service of the Lord,"* 199.

38. Alan Young notes that "the 'jubilee' emphasis on a smooth sound with sweet harmonies and often no definable lead singer was replaced by the 'hard quartets'—groups led by one or two powerful lead singers and aiming to 'wreck the house' by producing such an overpowering performance that the audience was reduced to shouting hysteria" (*Woke Me Up This Morning*, xxvi).

39. Darden, *People Get Ready*, 235.

40. R. Allen, *Singing in the Spirit*, 147.

41. These efforts to control the audience are even more important for blind performers than for the sighted. Jeffrey Peisch describes Stevie Wonder's frequent and often surprisingly urgent demands for audience response during his performances: "Stevie has always insisted that the people 'get into' his concerts, because if he doesn't hear their response he has no way of knowing if they're enjoying themselves" (*Stevie Wonder*, 51).

42. Heilbut, *Gospel Sound*, 347. The Blind Boys of Alabama most recently assayed these roles in a New York City production in 2004.

CHAPTER 4

1. Stadler, *Troubling Minds*, xvi.

2. Collier, *The Making of Jazz*, 141.

3. Stewart, *Jazz Masters of the 30s*, 184.

4. Marcus Roberts (b. 1963) is the best-known blind pianist currently active in American jazz. Although he won the National Association of Jazz Educators jazz competition in 1987 and was the first winner of the Thelonious Monk International Jazz Piano competition, professionally Marcus Roberts has received the most attention from his connection to Wynton Marsalis, who for more than twenty years has been the most powerful figure in the world of jazz.

5. Mancuso, *Popular Music and the Underground*, 274.

6. For instance, upon Charlie Parker's emergence onto the 1940s jazz scene, while there was almost immediate recognition of the scope of his talent, his strongest competitors often went to great lengths to make it clear that they had developed their styles independent of any knowledge of or influence from Parker's playing.

7. Reflecting with an even more pointed explicitness the awareness among his peers of Tatum's essential limitations as a competitor, one white musician supposedly responded to his first exposure to Tatum by crying out, "Good God! This Tatum is the greatest! Thank God he's black—otherwise nobody's job would be safe" (quoted in Stewart, *Jazz Masters of the 30s*, 190).

8. Schuller, *Swing Era,* 477.

9. In 1950, this genius would be immortalized in the fourteen-LP collection bluntly entitled *The Genius of Art Tatum.*

10. Hodeir, *Toward Jazz,* 131.

11. Keepnews, *View from Within,* 75. For a detailed review of Tatum's medical and surgical history, see F. Spencer, *Jazz and Death,* 42–54.

12. As Gerard Goggin and Chrisopher Newell define this term, "cultural citizenship" refers to "the right and opportunity of citizens to participate in the cultural life of a society" (*Digital Disability,* 102). For considerations of the changing dynamics of black manhood, see Marriott, *On Black Men;* Booker, *"I Will Wear No Chain!"*

13. Titchkosky, *Disability, Self, and Society,* 77.

14. Lester, *Too Marvelous for Words,* 31. The implication of driving as a marker of independent manhood and social modernity is especially interesting when one contrasts it with Blind Boy Fuller's and Gary Davis's even more disturbing obsessions with guns and knives.

15. Keepnews, *View from Within,* 80.

16. The trombonist Steve Turre said of his stint working with Kirk: "He was brilliant, a genius. I thought he was worth all of the accolades, but a lot of people didn't understand it or else they were jealous—whatever reason, he was accused at times of being a gimmick. And I worked with him, and I felt his pain. When that happened, I would see how it would hurt his feelings so much" (quoted in Carver and Bernstein, *Jazz Profiles,* 110).

17. Santoro, *Dancing in Your Head,* 127.

18. Kruth, *Bright Moments,* 1.

19. Kun, *Audiotopia,* 117.

20. F. Davis, *Like Young,* 97. Leonard Feather writes, "His music is a valid blend of vitality, sophistication, humor, surprise and, once in a while, a harmonic touch of the avant-garde" (*Book of Jazz,* 144).

21. Interestingly, before switching to the keyboard, the blind pianist and musical theoretician Lennie Tristano (1919–78) also performed such vaudeville tricks. Ira Gitler writes, "He worked with an accordion player in a group where he alternated between blowing two saxophones or three clarinets at once" (*Jazz Masters of the Forties,* 229). Few blind artists would as self-consciously fashion themselves as "thinkers" as did Lennie Tristano, whose status as someone in "the front rank of underappreciated 'genius' types in jazz" has been as widely disseminated and as consistently challenged as that of Ray Charles (Mancuso, *Popular Music and the Underground,* 367).

22. Kruth, *Bright Moments,* 101.

23. Forrest, *Relocations of the Spirit,* 343.

24. Another way in which Kirk gave his blindness, as a component of his public persona, a degree of centrality greater than that of most other blind performers was his tendency to actively seek out and perform and record with other blind musicians. One such performer, with whom Kirk had a notably productive relationship, was the singer Al Hibbler. Interestingly, like Kirk, Al Hibbler was also regularly accused by his detractors of having fashioned an essentially freakish and unmusical style.

25. Mendl, *Appeal of Jazz,* 134.

26. For an engaging and comprehensive consideration of this process across a range of popular culture forms, see Wynter, *American Skin.*

27. For instance, Clarence Carter was one of a few blind R & B artists to achieve significant success after the heyday of the blind blues performers in the 1920s and 1930s. His hits, the biggest of which was the melodramatic "Patches," represent a transitional musical persona between that of artists like Blind Lemon Jefferson and Blind Willie McTell and modern artists like Ray Charles and Stevie Wonder. Carter later revitalized his career by moving into the world of small-label R & B with hits like the salacious "Strokin'."

28. Cholden, *Psychiatrist Works with Blindness,* 97. The ability of blind performers like Charles and, later, Stevie Wonder to avoid being seen in public with canes, guide dogs, or other prosthetic markers of blindness has a normalizing function similar to the extreme lengths to which President Roosevelt went to prevent general knowledge of the extent of his disability during his terms in office. For an account of these efforts to hide the extent of Roosevelt's impairment, see Gallagher, *FDR's Splendid Deception.*

29. Charles's most notable gesture of deaf activism was his establishing of the Robinson Foundation for Hearing Disorders. As he explained this manifestly eccentric gesture: "My ears tell me 99 percent of what I need to know about my world. . . . My eyes are my handicap, but my ears are my opportunity" (Mathis, *Ray Charles,* n.p.).

30. Lydon, *Ray Charles,* 56. Ironically, one of only two known photographs of Blind Lemon Jefferson was similarly subjected to the addition of painted-on spectacles in order to normalize the image of the artist.

31. Charles and Ritz, *Brother Ray,* 116

32. Charles and Ritz, *Brother Ray,* 37

33. Charles and Ritz, *Brother Ray,* 41

34. Though figures like Edward Ellington, Aretha Franklin, and James Brown were variously the Duke, the Queen, and the King, Ray Charles was "the High Priest of the Blues" or, more simply, "Brother Ray." Tellingly, Charles both fostered and undercut this spiritualized image by entitling his autobiography *Brother Ray.* During the 1920s and 1930s, "Brother" was the term used by some secular blues singers when they recorded religious songs, thereby implying that—for the extent of that recording at least—their sins were somehow under erasure.

35. Shaw, *Honkers and Shouters,* 380.

36. Ritz, "Blues Is the Blood," 276.

37. This is equally true of the almost unrelentingly disturbing image of Charles as a philandering husband and tyrannical employer that one finds in Michael Lydon's *Ray Charles.*

38. Murray, *Stomping the Blues,* 30.

39. Murray, *Stomping the Blues,* 36.

40. Williams's statement reflects a fraudulent bit of press-agentry that was used to ground early attempts to pinpoint the relation between Charles's music and contemporary gospel. Charles freely admitted that Archie Brownlee of the Five Blind Boys of Mississippi had been a huge influence on his style, and near the beginning of his career publicity agents circulated the story that the singer had actu-

ally been a member of the Five Blind Boys. Charles quickly squelched this misrepresentation, however, not only because it was untrue but perhaps because he realized that it made him seem an even greater apostate (Ferris, *Blues from the Delta*, 80). As Viv Broughton puts it, "For many people, Ray Charles is the greatest gospel singer who never was" (*Black Gospel*, 100).

41. Watley, "Tradition of Worship," 291.

42. Teresa L. Reed writes, "Since the 1940s a firsthand, formative experience with music in the black church has been a virtual prerequisite for success in the world of rhythm and blues" (*Holy Profane*, 93).

43. P. Oliver, *Story of the Blues*, 145.

44. It was, in fact, Charles's passage through the world of country and western music that played a catalytic role in reestablishing and solidifying his status as a "genius" after his similarly appropriative engagement with the sound of black gospel had been absorbed into the mainstream of African American popular music (Southern, *Music of Black Americans*, 520).

45. For a consideration of mainstream America's rediscovery of Charles, see Wynter, *American Skin*, 126–29.

46. Lydon, *Ray Charles*, 236. Charles himself offered an interesting comment on one of the possible reasons for the waning of his record sales by the mid-1960s: "Since I couldn't see people dancing, the dance crazes passed me by" (Charles and Ritz, *Brother Ray*, 177). Despite its manifest plausibility, this statement does not address the fact that this period saw the record-buying public's acceptance of Stevie Wonder, an artist who was just as incapable as Charles of seeing people dancing.

47. One of the most notable of these artists was Solomon Burke, whose country-western-inflected hit "Just Out of Reach" sold over a million copies a year before Charles's album was released.

48. Charles and Ritz, *Brother Ray*, 72.

49. Turk, *Ray Charles*, 104.

50. These are the records *The Genius of Ray Charles* (1959), *Genius Hits the Road* (1960), *The Genius after Hours* (1961), *The Genius Sings the Blues* (1961), and *Genius Plus Soul Equals Jazz* (1961). The PBS/Masters of American Music documentary on Charles's life and career was entitled *Ray Charles: The Genius of Soul*. Mike Evans reports that "the 'Genius' tag was the invention of Jerry Wexler and, although Ray preferred other nicknames he'd begun to acquire—churchy titles like The High Priest and Brother Ray—it stuck" (*Ray Charles*, 121).

51. Petra Kuppers points out, "Performers can perform disability, and this performance has currency, tradition and weight in the social sphere of popular culture: film actors playing disabled characters have carried off a number of Oscars, making it seem that acting disabled is the highest achievement possible" (*Disability and Contemporary Performance*, 12).

52. Deborah Marks observes that "perhaps the real reason for not employing disabled people is that it is reassuring for the viewer to know that 'it's only pretend.' . . . Disabled characters function as objects available to receive the projections of non-disabled viewers, who can observe them from a safe distance. . . . As such, portrayals of disability are cathartic, offering a way for non-disabled people to express their fears and fantasies of lack, dependency and loss at one remove" (*Disability*, 160).

CHAPTER 5

1. Howe, *Genius Explained,* 130.

2. R. Ochse writes that "prodigies are the product of an interacting set of forces, including natural capacity, parental interest and effort, and appropriate introduction to the relevant domain" (*Before the Gates of Excellence,* 163). For a general overview of the child-prodigy phenomenon, see Radford, *Child Prodigies.*

3. Quoted in G. Mitchell, "Stevie Wonder," 19.

4. Reed, *Holy Profane,* 94.

5. Although his was not nearly as well-funded or intensive, Ray Charles received similar training during his years as a student at the Florida School for the Deaf and Blind.

6. Hull and Stahel, *Wonder Years,* 169–70.

7. Elsner, *Stevie Wonder,* 24.

8. Lowenfeld, *Berthold Lowenfeld on Blindness and Blind People,* 38.

9. F. Spencer, *Jazz and Death,* 43. According to James Haskins and Kathleen Benson, "this condition left approximately 12,000 children born during the Forties and early Fifties blind" (*Stevie Wonder Scrapbook,* 10).

10. Koestler, *Unseen Minority,* 415.

11. Writing in 1972, Philip Hatlen observed that "the rate of unemployment is unbelievable, when you consider the skills and the capacity of some of these young people" ("Educational Research," 40).

12. Haskins and Benson, *Stevie Wonder Scrapbook,* 54.

13. Gordy, *To Be Loved,* 148. An alternative account of the provenance of Wonder's stage name is the claim that "when he was twelve years old, Stevie composed two concertos. When he played them for his conductor Clarence Paul, and others at Hitsville, they started calling him the little boy wonder" (Haskins and Benson, *Stevie Wonder Scrapbook,* 34).

14. Bogdan, *Freak Show,* 212.

15. Gordy, *To Be Loved,* 148.

16. Merish, "Cuteness and Commodity Aesthetics," 187.

17. Merish, "Cuteness and Commodity Aesthetics," 188.

18. Lee Edelman writes that "cuteness enables a general misrecognition of sexuality (which always implicitly endangers ideals of sociality and communal enjoyment) as, at least in the dominant form of heterosexual reproduction, securing the collective reality it otherwise threatens to destroy" (*No Future,* 137).

19. This would also be true of Motown's later investment in its other child superstar, Michael Jackson.

20. Hull and Stahel, *Wonder Years,* 39.

21. James E. Perone usefully points out that "it is important to note that Wonder has focused not on the dime-store-variety harmonica, nor on the blues harp, but on the chromatic harmonica, a more difficult instrument to play but also one that can be adapted to a far greater range of musical styles because of both its melodic nature and its ability to play pitches that are absent from the simpler types of harmonicas" (*Sound of Stevie Wonder,* 3).

22. Although in his case certainly appropriate, the appellation "Little" was not unique to Wonder or even particularly rare in black popular music. African Amer-

ican performers who bore the tag "little" at some point in their career include Little Brother Montgomery, Little Walter Jacobs, Little Milton Campbell, Little Esther Phillips, and—most famously—Little Richard Penniman.

23. Quoted in Elsner, *Stevie Wonder,* 47.

24. Lydon, *Ray Charles,* 225.

25. Wynter, *American Skin,* 2.

26. Quoted in G. Mitchell, "Stevie Wonder," 19.

27. G. Mitchell, "Stevie Wonder," 15.

28. White, *Rock Lives,* 209.

29. White, *Rock Lives,* 209.

30. Haskins and Benson, *Stevie Wonder Scrapbook,* 149.

31. Quoted in S. Davis, *Stevie Wonder,* 95.

32. Quoted in Elsner, *Stevie Wonder,* 148.

33. Quoted in G. Mitchell, "Stevie Wonder," 18.

34. John Howard Griffin, author of *Black Like Me,* a writer who specialized in attempting to see things from the perspective of "the other," wrote in his memoir of the ten years that he spent as a completely blind man after receiving a brain injury in combat in World War II: "Blindness isolates a man; he never sees ugliness at very close range. Contacts are usually limited to those who modulate information for his benefit. His isolation from externals—the hardening surface of a society—is much more complete than the sighted imagine" (*Scattered Shadows,* 154). In Wonder's case, this tendency to "see" the bright side of things may also have been fostered and reinforced by the sheltered life that he experienced after he came within the Motown orbit.

35. See Gates, *Signifying Monkey.*

36. Sanello, *Eddie Murphy,* 97.

37. Hull and Stahel, *Wonder Years,* 36.

38. Love and Brown, *Blind Faith,* 144. Wonder himself has said: "When you're blind you build up a lot of energy that other people get rid of through their eyes. Blind people have to work it off some other way and it is an unconscious thing.... Everybody develops their own blindism" (quoted in Elsner, *Stevie Wonder,* 57).

39. Fox-Cumming, *Stevie Wonder,* 38.

40. Quoted in G. Mitchell, "Stevie Wonder," 18–19.

41. Hillyer, *Feminism and Disability,* 116.

42. Elsner, *Stevie Wonder,* 90.

43. This commitment has been revealed most notably by his sponsorship of the Stevie Wonder Home for Blind and Retarded Children, which he established in 1976.

44. Haskins and Benson, *Stevie Wonder Scrapbook,* 92–93.

45. Deborah Marks writes of this type of "disability simulation": "Simulation exercises attempt to give non-disabled people an insight into the experience of impairment. . . . However, such training often fails to capture some of the most difficult aspects of their impairment, such as the effect of cumulative frustration, pain, fatigue or social isolation. On the other hand, simulation can also over-estimate some aspects of difficulties. . . . Rather than listening to what disabled people are saying, simulation may pander to voyeuristic excitement and give non-disabled people the opportunity to colonise the experience of disability" (*Disability,* 134).

46. R. Scott, *Making of Blind Men,* 37.

47. Before the boom in the awareness of "Latin" music among non-Latin audiences, it may have been the lack of significant corporate investment in exploiting his potential that led to the more limited success of the blind Puerto Rican guitarist José Feliciano, who never managed to sustain the momentum created by his hugely successful recording "Light My Fire."

48. Quoted in Elsner, *Stevie Wonder,* 341.

49. Quoted in Elsner, *Stevie Wonder,* 96.

50. Horn, *Innervisions,* 238.

51. Nirmana Erevelles writes, "Those disabled people who face economic deprivation on a daily basis seldom have access to the technology that can offer their 'unlivable' bodies the cyborgean possibilities that poststructuralists extol" ("In Search of the Disabled Subject," 98).

52. Quoted in Swenson, *Stevie Wonder,* 131.

53. Perone, *Sound of Stevie Wonder,* 34.

54. SAP stands for Systems, Applications, and Products in Data Processing. Indicating once again his ability to provide contexts that make his condition as a person with a disability understandable and unthreatening to the unimpaired, Wonder, at the SAP awards ceremony, joked, "The real reason that I got involved in this whole thing was because, I figure, about two years from now, I'd like to be driving" (T. Williams, *Stevie Wonder,* 84).

55. Quoted in T. Williams, *Stevie Wonder,* 84.

Bibliography

Abbington, James, ed. *Readings in African American Church Music and Worship.* Chicago: GIA Publications, 2001.

Abbott, Lynn, and Doug Seroff. *Out of Sight: The Rise of African American Popular Music, 1889–1895.* Jackson: University Press of Mississippi, 2002.

A'Becket, John. "Blind Tom as He Is Today." *Black Perspective in Music* 4, no. 2 (1976): 184–88.

Abrahams, Yvette. "Images of Sara Bartman: Sexuality, Race, and Gender in Early–Nineteenth-Century Britain." In *Nation, Empire, Colony: Historicizing Gender and Race,* ed. Ruth Roach Pierson and Nupur Chaudhuri, 220–36. Bloomington: Indiana University Press, 1998.

Abu-Habib, Lina. "Working with Disabled Women: Reviewing Our Approach." In *Gender and Disability: Women's Experiences in the Middle East,* ed. Lina Abu-Habib, 9–25. Oxford: Oxfam, 1997.

Adams, Bluford. *E Pluribus Barnum: The Great Showman and the Making of U.S. Popular Culture.* Minneapolis: University of Minnesota Press, 1997.

Adams, Rachel. *Sideshow U.S.A.: Freaks and the American Cultural Imagination.* Chicago: University of Chicago Press, 2001.

Ainlay, Stephen Charles. *Day Brought Back My Night: Aging and New Vision Loss.* London: Routledge, 1989.

Allen, Brenda J. *Difference Matters: Communicating Social Identity.* Long Grove, IL: Waveland Press, 2004.

Allen, Ray. *Singing in the Spirit: African-American Sacred Quartets in New York City.* Philadelphia: University of Pennsylvania Press, 1991.

Anderson, Eric D. "Black Responses to Darwinism, 1859–1915." In *Disseminating Darwinism: The Role of Place, Race, Religion, and Gender,* ed. Ronald L. Numbers and John Stenhouse, 247–66. Cambridge: Cambridge University Press, 1999.

Aschoff, Peter R. "The Poetry of the Blues: Understanding the Blues in Its Cultural Context." In Jones and Jones, *Triumph of the Soul,* 35–67.

Backer, Matt. "The Guitar." In Moore, *Cambridge Companion to Blues and Gospel Music,* 116–29.

Baldwin, James. *The Price of the Ticket: Collected Nonfiction, 1948–1985.* New York: St. Martin's/Marek, 1985.

Barasch, Moshe. *Blindness: The History of a Mental Image in Western Thought.* New York: Routledge, 2001.

Barlow, William. *Looking Up at Down: The Emergence of Blues Culture.* Philadelphia: Temple University Press, 1989.

Barnes, Colin, Geof Mercer, and Tom Shakespeare. *Exploring Disability: A Sociological Introduction.* Cambridge: Polity Press, 1999.

Bastin, Bruce. *Red River Blues: The Blues Tradition in the Southeast.* Urbana: University of Illinois Press, 1986.

Bastin, Bruce. "Truckin' My Blues Away: East Coast Piedmont Styles." In Cohn, *Nothin' but the Blues,* 205–31.

Battersby, Jack A. *Blind Boone: Missouri's Ragtime Pioneer.* Columbia: University of Missouri Press, 1998.

Baynton, Douglas C. "Disability and the Justification of Inequality in American History." In *New Disability History,* 33–57.

Beardsley, Edward H. *A History of Neglect: Health Care for Blacks and Mill Workers in the Twentieth-Century South.* Knoxville: University of Tennessee Press, 1987.

Beyer, Mark. *Stevie Wonder: Rock and Roll Hall of Famers.* New York: Rosen Publishing Group, 2002.

Black, Edwin. *War against the Weak: Eugenics and America's Campaign to Create a Master Race.* New York: Four Walls, Eight Windows, 2003.

"'Blind Tom,' A Musical Prodigy." *London Daily News,* 3 July 1866. http://www .twainquotes.com/brochure.html. Accessed 20 March 2003.

"'Blind Tom,' The Negro Pianist." *Albany (NY) Argus,* January 1866. http://www .twainquotes. com/brochure.html. Accessed 20 March 2003.

Blumhofer, Edith L. *Her Heart Can See: The Life and Hums of Fanny J. Crosby.* Grand Rapids: Wm. B. Eerdmans Publishing Co., 2005.

Boeckmann, Cathy. *A Question of Character: Scientific Racism and the Genres of American Fiction, 1892–1912.* Tuscaloosa: University of Alabama Press, 2000.

Bogdan, Robert. *Freak Show: Presenting Human Oddities for Amusement and Profit.* Chicago: University of Chicago Press, 1988.

Bogdan, Robert. "The Social Construction of Freaks." In Thomson, *Freakery,* 23–37.

Booker, Christopher B. *"I Will Wear No Chain!": A Social History of African American Males.* Westport, CT: Praeger, 2000.

Boulter, Eric. "Living with Blindness." In Dobree and Boulter, *Blindness and Visual Handicap,* 111–225.

Boyer, Horace Clarence. "A Comparative Analysis of Traditional and Contemporary Gospel Music." In Jackson, *More Than Dancing,* 128–46.

Boyer, Horace Clarence. *How Sweet the Sound: The Golden Age of Gospel.* Washington, DC: Elliot and Clark Publishing, 1995.

Branson, Jan, and Don Miller. *Damned for Their Difference: The Cultural Construction of Deaf People as Disabled.* Washington, DC: Gallaudet University Press, 2002.

Broughton, Viv. *Black Gospel: An Illustrated History of the Gospel Sound.* Poole: Blandford Press, 1984.

Bullock, Penelope L. *The Afro-American Periodical Press, 1838–1909.* Baton Rouge: Louisiana State University Press, 1981.

Bunch, William. "The Slave and the Doctor's Son." *Brown Alumni Magazine Online,* September–October 2001. http://brownalumnimagazine.com/storydetail.cfm ?iD=289. Accessed 20 March 2003.

Bunch, William. "Strange Harmonies." *American Legacy* 9, no. 4 (2004): 16–24.

Burlingham, Dorothy. *Psychoanalytic Studies of the Sighted and the Blind.* New York: International Universities Press, 1972.

Burnim, Mellonee V. "The Black Gospel Music Tradition: A Complex of Ideology, Aesthetic, and Behavior." In Jackson, *More Than Dancing,* 147–67.

Byrd, Michael W., and Linda A. Clayton. *An American Health Dilemma: A Medical History of African Americans and the Problem of Race, Beginnings to 1900.* New York: Routledge, 2000.

Cabbil, Lila, and Moniqueka E. Gold. "African Americans with Visual Impairments." In Milian and Erin, *Diversity and Visual Impairment,* 57–77.

Cahill, Madeleine A., and Martin F. Norden. "Hollywood's Portrayal of Disabled Women." In Hans and Patri, *Women, Disability, and Identity,* 56–75.

Canguilhem, Georges. *The Normal and the Pathological.* Trans. Carolyn R. Fawcett and Robert S. Cohen. New York: Zone Books, 1989.

Carr, Roy. "Jazz Festivals." In *A Century of Jazz,* ed. Roy Carr, 228–35. 1997. London: Hamlyn Press, 2004.

Carrothers, James D. "Blind Tom, Singing." *Southern Workman* 30, no. 5 (1901): 258–59.

Carver, Reginald, and Lenny Bernstein. *Jazz Profiles: The Spirit of the Nineties.* New York: Billboard Books, 1998.

Cather, Willa. *My Ántonia.* 1819. Ed. Charles Mignon and Kari Ronning. Lincoln: University of Nebraska Press, 1994.

Charles, Ray, and David Ritz. *Brother Ray: Ray Charles' Own Story.* 1978. New York: Da Capo Press, 1992.

Charters, Samuel B. *The Country Blues.* 1959. New York: Da Capo Press, 1975.

Charters, Samuel B. *The Legacy of the Blues.* 1975. New York Da Capo Press, 1977.

Charters, Samuel B. *Sweet as the Showers of Rain: The Bluesmen, Volume II.* London: Oak Publications, 1977.

Chenu, Bruno. *The Trouble I've Seen: The Big Book of Negro Spirituals.* Trans. Eugene V. LaPlante. Valley Forge, PA: Judson Press, 2003.

Chevigny, Hector, and Sydell Braverman. *The Adjustment of the Blind.* New Haven: Yale University Press, 1950.

Cholden, Louis S. *A Psychiatrist Works with Blindness: Selected Papers.* New York: American Foundation for the Blind, 1958.

Clayton, Lawrence, and Joe W. Specht, eds. *The Roots of Texas Music.* College Station: Texas A&M Press, 2003.

Cohen, Oscar. "Prejudice and the Blind." In Lukoff et al., *Attitudes toward Blind Persons,* 16–34.

Cohen, Ronald D. *Rainbow Quest: The Folk Music Revival and American Society, 1940–1970.* Amherst: University of Massachusetts Press, 2002.

Cohn, Lawrence, ed. *Nothin' but the Blues: The Music and the Musicians.* New York: Abbeville Press, 1993.

Collier, James Lincoln. *The Making of Jazz: A Comprehensive History.* New York: Dell Publishing Co., 1978.

Cook, James W., Jr. "Of Men, Missing Links, and Nondescripts: The Strange Career of P. T. Barnum's 'What Is It?' Exhibition." In Thomson, *Freakery,* 139–57.

Cone, James H. *The Spirituals and the Blues: An Interpretation.* 1972. Maryknoll, NY: Orbis Books, 1991.

Corker, Mairian. *Deaf and Disabled, or Deafness Disabled? Towards a Human Rights Perspective.* Buckingham: Open University Press, 1998.

Cornoldi, Cesare, and Tomaso Vecchi. "Mental Imagery in Blind People: The Role of Passive and Active Visuospatial Processes." In *Touch, Representation, and Blindness,* ed. Morton A. Heller, 143–82. Oxford: Oxford University Press, 2000.

Covey, Herbert C. *Social Perceptions of People with Disabilities in History.* Springfield, IL: Charles C. Thomas Publisher, 1998.

Cowen, Tyler. *Creative Destruction: How Globalization Is Changing the World's Cultures.* Princeton: Princeton University Press, 2002.

Cowley, John H. "Don't Leave Me Here: Non-commercial Blues: The Field Trips, 1924–60." In Cohn, *Nothin' but the Blues,* 265–345.

Cruz, Jon. *Culture on the Margins: The Black Spiritual and the Rise of American Cultural Interpretation.* Princeton: Princeton University Press, 1999.

Csikszentmihalyi, Mihaly. "Creativity and Genius: A Systems Perspective." In Steptoe, *Genius and the Mind,* 39–64.

Cusic, Don. *The Sound of Light: A History of Gospel Music.* Bowling Green, OH: Bowling Green State University Popular Press, 1990.

Cutsforth, Thomas D. *The Blind in School and Society: A Psychological Study.* New York: D. Appleton and Company, 1933.

Darden, Robert. *People Get Ready: A New History of Black Gospel Music.* New York: Continuum, 2004.

Davis, Angela. *Blues Legacies and Black Feminism: Gertrude "Ma" Rainey, Bessie Smith, and Billie Holiday.* New York: Pantheon Books, 1998.

Davis, Francis. *The History of the Blues: The Roots, The Music, The People from Charley Patton to Robert Cray.* New York: Hyperion, 1995.

Davis, Francis. *Like Young: Jazz, Pop, Youth, and Middle Age.* Cambridge: Da Capo Press, 2001.

Davis, Lennard J. *Bending Over Backwards: Disability, Dismodernism, and Other Difficult Positions.* New York: New York University Press, 2002.

Davis, Lennard J. *Enforcing Normalcy: Disability, Deafness, and the Body.* London: Verso, 1995.

Davis, Rebecca Harding. "Blind Tom." In *A Rebecca Harding Davis Reader,* ed. Jean Pfaelzer, 104–11. Pittsburgh: University of Pittsburgh Press, 1995.

Davis, Sharon. *Stevie Wonder: Rhythms of Wonder.* London: Robson Books, 2003.

de Lerma, Dominique-René. "Introduction." In *Blind Tom, the Black Pianist-Composer (1849–1908): Continually Enslaved,* by Geneva Handy Southall. Lanhan, MD: Scarecrow Press, 1999.

Dicaire, David. *Blues Singers: Biographies of 50 Legendary Artists of the Early 20th Century.* Jefferson, NC, and London: McFarland and Company, 1999.

Dignani, Vanda. "Women, Affectivity, Handicaps." In Hans and Patri, *Women, Disability, and Identity,* 129–36.

"Dispute over Blind Tom. Several Persons at Funeral Deny That Body Was That of Musician." *New York Times,* 16 June 1908. http://www.twainquotes.com/Tom Obit.html. Accessed 20 March 2003.

Dixon, Christa K. *Negro Spirituals: From Bible to Folk Song.* Philadelphia: Fortress Press, 1976.

Dobree, John. H. "Causes of Blindness." In Dobree and Boulter, *Blindness and Visual Handicap,* 5–109.

Dobree, John H., and Eric Boulter, eds. *Blindness and Visual Handicap: The Facts.* Oxford: Oxford University Press, 1982.

Dupree, Sherry Sherrod, and Herbert C. Dupree. *African-American Good News (Gospel) Music.* Washington, DC: Middle Atlantic Regional Press, 1993.

Edelman, Lee. *No Future: Queer Theory and the Death Drive.* Durham: Duke University Press, 2004.

Elsner, Constanze. *Stevie Wonder.* New York: Popular Library, 1977.

Erevelles, Nirmala. "In Search of the Disabled Subject." In Wilson and Lewiecki-Wilson, *Embodied Rhetorics,* 92–111.

Erin, Jane N. "Individual and Societal Responses to Diversity and Visual Impairment." In Milian and Erin, *Diversity and Visual Impairment,* 3–33.

Erin, Jane N., and Madeline Milian. "Professionals and Diversity." In Milian and Erin, *Diversity and Visual Impairment,* 383–412.

Evans, David. *Big Road Blues: Tradition and Creativity in the Folk Blues.* Berkeley and Los Angeles: University of California Press, 1982.

Evans, David. "Goin' Up the Country: Blues in Texas and the Deep South." In Cohn, *Nothin' but the Blues,* 33–86.

Evans, David. "Musical Innovation in the Blues of Blind Lemon Jefferson." *Black Music Research Journal* 20, no. 1 (2000): 83–109.

Evans, Mike. *Ray Charles: The Birth of Soul.* London: Omnibus Press, 2005.

Ezra, Elizabeth. *The Colonial Unconscious: Race and Culture in Interwar France.* Ithaca: Cornell University Press, 2000.

Farley, Christopher John. "Visionary Blindness: Blind Lemon Jefferson and Other Vision-Impaired Bluesmen." In Guralnick et al., *Martin Scorsese Presents the Blues,* 165–70.

Farrell, Gabriel. *The Story of Blindness.* Cambridge: Harvard University Press, 1956.

Feather, Leonard. *The Book of Jazz: From Then till Now.* New York: Bonanza Books, 1965.

Ferris, William. *Blues from the Delta.* Garden City, NY: Anchor Press/ Doubleday, 1978.

Fett, Sharla M. *Working Cures: Healing, Health, and Power on Southern Slave Plantations.* Chapel Hill: University of North Carolina Press, 2002.

Fine, Michelle, and Adrienne Asch. "Disability beyond Stigma: Social Interaction, Discrimination, and Activism." In Rosenblum and Travis, *Meaning of Difference,* 201–9.

Finsestone, Samuel, ed. *Social Casework and Blindness.* New York: American Foundation for the Blind, 1960.

Floyd, Samuel A., Jr. *International Dictionary of Black Composers, Volume 1.* Chicago: Fitzroy Dearborn Publishers, 1999.

Forrest, Leon. *Relocations of the Spirit.* Wakefield, RI: Asphodel Press, 1994.

Fox-Cumming, Ray. *Stevie Wonder.* Suffolk: Mandabrook Books, 1977.

Frame, Melissa. *Blind Spots: The Communicative Performance of Visual Impairment in Relationships and Social Interaction.* Springfield, IL: Charles C. Thomas, 2004.

Freeberg, Ernest. *The Education of Laura Bridgman: First Deaf and Blind Person to Learn Language.* Cambridge: Harvard University Press, 2001.

French, Richard Slayton. *From Homer to Helen Keller: A Social and Educational Study of the Blind.* New York: American Foundation for the Blind, 1932.

French, Sally, and John Swain. *From a Different Viewpoint: The Lives and Experiences of Visually Impaired People.* London: Royal National Institute for the Blind, 1997.

Frost, Linda. *Never One Nation: Freaks, Savages, and Whiteness in U.S. Popular Culture, 1850–1877.* Minneapolis: University of Minnesota Press, 2005.

Fuell, Melissa. *Blind Boone: His Early Life and His Achievements.* Kansas City: Burton Publishing Co., 1915.

Gallagher, Hugh Gregory. *FDR's Splendid Deception.* New York: Dodd, Mead, 1985.

Gamble, Vanessa Northington, ed. *Germs Have No Color Line: Blacks and American Medicine, 1900–1940.* New York: Garland Publishing, 1989.

Garland, Robert. *The Eye of the Beholder: Deformity and Disability in the Graeco-Roman World.* Ithaca: Cornell University Press, 1995.

Garon, Paul. *Blues and the Poetic Spirit.* 1975. San Francisco: City Lights, 1996.

Gates, Henry Louis, Jr. *The Signifying Monkey: A Theory of Afro-American Literary Criticism.* New York: Oxford University Press, 1988.

George, Luvenia A. "Lucie E. Campbell: Her Nurturing and Expansion of Gospel Music in the National Baptist Convention U.S.A., Inc." In Reagon, *We'll Understand It Better By and By,* 109–19.

Gerber, David A. "Blind and Enlightened: The Contested Origins of the Egalitarian Politics of the Blinded Veterans Association." In *New Disability History,* 313–34.

Gerber, David A. "The 'Careers' of People Exhibited in Freak Shows: The Problem of Volition and Valorization." In Thomson, *Freakery,* 38–54.

Geremek, Bronislaw. *Poverty: A History.* Oxford: Blackwell, 1994.

Gitler, Ira. *Jazz Masters of the Forties.* 1966. New York: Da Capo Press, 1983.

Gitter, Elisabeth. *The Imprisoned Guest: Samuel Howe and Laura Bridgman, the Original Deaf-Blind Girl.* New York: Farrar, Straus and Giroux, 2001.

Glasgow Daily Herald, 2 January 1867. http://www.twainquotes.com/brochure.html. Accessed 3 March 2003.

Goff, James R., Jr. *Close Harmony: A History of Southern Gospel.* Chapel Hill: University of North Carolina Press, 2002.

Goggin, Gerard, and Christopher Newell. *Digital Disability: The Social Construction of Disability in New Media.* Lanham, MD: Rowman and Littlefield Publishers, 2003.

Goode, David. *A World without Words: The Social Construction of Children Born Deaf and Blind.* Philadelphia: Temple University Press, 1994.

Goodley, Dan, and Rebecca Lawthom, eds. *Disability and Psychology: Critical Introductions and Reflections.* New York: Palgrave Macmillan 2006.

Gordy, Berry. *To Be Loved: The Music, the Magic, the Memories of Motown.* New York: Warner Books, 1994.

Goreau, Laurraine. *Just Mahalia Baby: The Mahalia Jackson Story.* 1975. Gretna, LA: Pelican Publishing Company, 1984.

Gottschalk, Louis Moreau. *Notes of a Pianist.* Ed. Jeanne Behrend. New York: Da Capo Press, 1979.

Govenar, Alan. "Blind Lemon Jefferson: The Myth and the Man." *Black Music Research Journal* 20, no. 1 (2000): 7–21.

Govenar, Alan. "That Black Snake Moan: The Music and Mystery of Blind Lemon Jefferson." In Welding and Byron, *Bluesland,* 16–37.

Govenar, Alan B., and Jay F. Brakefield. *Deep Ellum and Central Track: Where the*

Black and White Worlds of Dallas Converged. Denton: University of North Texas Press, 1998.

Grabs, Long. "Untitled." *Fayetteville Observer,* 19 May 1862. http://www.twainquotes.com/blindtom.html. Accessed 20 March 2003.

Graham, Milton D., ed. *Science and Blindness: Retrospective and Prospective.* New York: American Foundation for the Blind, 1972.

Green, Benny. *The Reluctant Art: Five Studies in the Growth of Jazz.* 1962. New York: Da Capo Press, 1991.

Griffin, John Howard. *Scattered Shadows: A Memoir of Blindness and Vision.* Maryknoll, NY: Orbis Books, 2004.

Grob, Gerald N. *The Deadly Truth: A History of Disease in America.* Cambridge: Harvard University Press, 2002.

Groom, Bob. *The Blues Revival.* London: Studio Vista, 1971.

Grosz, Elizabeth. "Intolerable Ambiguity: Freaks as/at the Limit." In Thomson, *Freakery,* 55–66.

Guattari, Félix. *Molecular Revolution: Psychiatry and Politics.* Trans. Rosemary Shedd. Middlesex: Penguin Books, 1984.

Guralnick, Peter, Robert Santelli, Holly George-Warren, and Christopher John Farley, eds. *Martin Scorsese Presents the Blues: A Musical Journey.* New York: Amistad, 2003.

Hagan, Chet. *Gospel Legends.* New York: Avon Books, 1995.

Hans, Asha, and Annie Patri, eds. *Women, Disability, and Identity.* New Delhi: Sage Publications, 2003.

Hansen, Barry. *Rhino's Cruise through the Blues.* San Francisco: Miller Freeman, 2000.

Harrah, Madge. *Blind Boone: Piano Prodigy.* Minneapolis: Carolrhoda Books, 2004.

Harris, Michael W. *The Rise of the Gospel Blues: The Music of Thomas Andrew Dorsey in the Urban Church.* New York: Oxford University Press, 1992.

Harris, Seale. "Tuberculosis in the Negro." In Gamble, *Germs Have No Color Line,* 1–5.

Hartman, Gary. "The Roots Run Deep: An Overview of Texas Music History." In Clayton and Specht, *Roots of Texas Music,* 3–36.

Haskins, James. *Black Music in America: A History through Its People.* New York: Thomas Y. Crowell Junior Books, 1987.

Haskins, James, and Kathleen Benson. *The Stevie Wonder Scrapbook.* London: Cassell, 1979.

Hatch, David, and Stephen Millward. *From Blues to Rock: An Analytical History of Pop Music.* Manchester: Manchester University Press, 1987.

Hatlen, Philip. "Educational Research and Severe Visual Impairment." In Graham, *Science and Blindness,* 29–51.

Hawkins, Mike. *Social Darwinism in European and American Thought, 1860–1945: Nature as Model and Nature as Threat.* Cambridge: Cambridge University Press, 1997.

Hayden, Deborah. *Pox: Genius, Madness, and the Mysteries of Syphilis.* New York: Basic Books, 2003.

Hayman, Robert L., Jr., and Nancy Levit. "Un-Natural Things: Constructions of Race, Gender, and Disability." In *Crossroads, Directions, and a New Critical Race*

Theory, ed. Francisco Valdes, Jerome McCristal Culp, and Angela P. Harris, 159–86. Philadelphia: Temple University Press, 2002.

Heilbut, Anthony. *The Gospel Sound: Good News and Bad Times.* 1971. New York: Limelight Editions, 1985.

Hendricks, Obery M., Jr. "'I Am the Holy Dope Dealer': The Problem with Gospel Music Today." In Abbington, *Readings in African American Church Music and Worship,* 553–89.

Henson, R. A. "Neurological Aspects of Musical Experience." In *Music and the Brain: Studies in the Neurology of Music,* ed. Macdonald Critchley and R. A. Henson, 3–21. London: William Heinemann Medical Books Limited, 1977.

Herder, Nicole Beaulieu, and Ronald Herder, eds. *Best-Loved Negro Spirituals: Complete Lyrics to 178 Songs of Faith.* Mineola, NY: Dover Publications, 2001.

Herrmann, Dorothy. *Helen Keller: A Life.* Chicago: University of Chicago Press, 1998.

Hillsman, Joan. *Gospel Music: An African American Art Form.* New York: McGraw-Hill Companies, 1998.

Hillyer, Barbara. *Feminism and Disability.* Norman: University of Oklahoma Press, 1993.

Hinson, Glenn. *Fire in My Bones: Transcendence and the Holy Spirit in African American Gospel.* Philadelphia: University of Pennsylvania Press, 2000.

Hobbs, June Haddon. *"I Sing for I Cannot Be Silent: The Feminization of American Hymnody, 1870–1920.* Pittsburgh: University of Pittsburgh Press, 1997.

Hobson, J. Allan. *Dreaming: An Introduction to the Science of Sleep.* Oxford: Oxford University Press, 2002.

Hodeir, André. *Toward Jazz.* Trans. Noel Burch. New York: Da Capo Press. 1962.

Hollins, Mark. *Understanding Blindness: An Integrative Approach.* Hillsdale, NJ: Lawrence Erlbaum Associates, 1989.

Holmes, Martha Stoddard. *Fictions of Affliction: Physical Disability in Victorian Culture.* Ann Arbor: University of Michigan Press, 2004.

Holmes, Zan W. "Encounter Jesus in Worship." In Abbington, *Readings in African American Church Music and Worship,* 327–37.

Horn, Martin E. *Innervisions: The Music of Stevie Wonder.* Bloomington: 1st Books, 2000.

Hoskyns, Barney, and David Stubbs. "The Boy Wonder." *Uncut,* Take 97, June 2005, 52–70.

Howe, Michael J. A. "Early Lives: Prodigies and Non-Prodigies." In Steptoe, *Genius and the Mind,* 97–109.

Howe, Michael J. A. *Fragments of Genius: The Strange Feats of Idiots Savants.* London: Routledge, 1989.

Howe, Michael J. A. *Genius Explained.* Cambridge: Cambridge University Press, 1999.

Huffman, David. "On Playing Don Baker in 'Butterflies Are Free.'" In Lukoff et al., *Attitudes toward Blind Persons,* 71–74.

Hull, John M. *In the Beginning There Was Darkness: A Blind Person's Conversations with the Bible.* Harrisburg, PA: Trinity Press, International, 2001.

Hull, John M. *On Sight and Insight: A Journey Into the World of Blindness.* Oxford: Oneworld Publications, 1997.

Hull, Ted, and Paula L. Stahel. *The Wonder Years: My Life and Times With Stevie Wonder.* Tampa: Ted Hull, 2000.

Humphrey, Mark. "Holy Blues: The Gospel Tradition." In Cohn, *Nothin' but the Blues,* 107–50.

Hurston, Zora Neale. "Spirituals and Neo-Spirituals." In *The Negro in Music and Art,* ed. Lindsay Patterson, 15–18. New York: Publishers Company, 1967.

Hutton, Frankie. *The Early Black Press in America, 1827–1860.* Westport, CT: Greenwood Publishing Group, 1993.

Jackson, Irene V. "Introduction." In Jackson, *More Than Dancing,* 3–7.

Jackson, Irene V., ed. *More Than Dancing: Essays on Afro-American Music and Musicians.* Westport, CT: Greenwood Press, 1985.

Jasen, David A., and Gene Jones. *Spreadin' Rhythm Around: Black Popular Songwiters, 1880–1930.* New York: Schirmer Books, 1998.

Jasen, David A., and Trebor Jay Tichenor. *Rags and Ragtime: A Musical History.* New York: Seabury Press, 1978.

Jay, Ricky. *Learned Pigs and Fireproof Women.* New York: Villard Books, 1986.

Jones, Arthur C. "Upon This Rock: The Foundational Influence of the Spirituals." In Jones and Jones, *Triumph of the Soul,* 3–34.

Jones, Arthur C. *Wade in the Water: The Wisdom of the Spirituals.* Maryknoll, NY: Orbis Books, 1993.

Jones, Bobby, and Lesley Sussman. *Touched by God: Black Gospel Greats Share Their Stories of Finding God.* New York: Pocket Books, 1998.

Jones, F. O., ed. "Blind Tom." In *A Handbook of American Music and Musicians,* 15. 1886. New York: Da Capo Press, 1971.

Jones, Ferdinand, and Arthur C. Jones, eds. *The Triumph of the Soul: Cultural and Psychological Aspects of African American Music.* Westport, CT: Praeger Publishers, 2001.

Jones, Gayl. *Corregidora.* Boston: Beacon Press, 1975.

Jones, James H. *Bad Blood: The Tuskegee Syphilis Experiment.* 1981. Expanded ed. New York: Free Press, 1993.

Jones, LeRoi (Amiri Baraka). *Blues People: Negro Music in White America.* 1963. Westport, CT: Greenwood Press, 1980.

Josephson, Eric. *The Social Life of Blind People.* New York: American Foundation for the Blind, 1968.

Jourdain, Robert. *Music, the Brain, and Ecstasy: How Music Captures Our Imagination.* New York: William Morrow and Company, 1997.

Joyner, Hannah. "This Unnatural and Fratricidal Strife: A Family's Negotiation of the Civil War, Deafness, and Independence." In *New Disability History,* 83–106.

Karfp, Juanita. "Art Music and Activist Discourse: The Case of the African-American Musician Amelia Tilghman." In *Nineteenth-Century Music: Selected Proceedings of the Tenth International Conference,* ed. Jim Samson and Bennett Zon, 335–44. Aldershot: Ashgate Publishing Company, 2002.

Keepnews, Orrin. *The View from Within: Jazz Writings, 1948–1987.* New York: Oxford University Press, 1988.

Keil, Charles. *Urban Blues.* Chicago and London: University of Chicago Press, 1966.

Kempton, Murray, and Arthur Kempton. "Big Joe Turner: The Holler of a Mountain Jack." In Welding and Byron, *Bluesland,* 114–29.

Kenneson, Claude, ed. *Musical Prodigies: Perilous Journeys, Remarkable Lives.* Portland, OR: Amadeus Press, 1998.

Kent, Drew. *Blind Lemon Jefferson: The 94 Classic Sides Remastered.* JSP Records, 2003.

Kiple, Kenneth F., and Virginia Himmelsteib King. *Another Dimension to the Black Diaspora: Diet, Disease, and Racism.* Cambridge: Cambridge University Press, 1981.

Kirtley, Donald D. *The Psychology of Blindness.* Chicago: Nelson-Hall Publishers, 1975.

Klages, Mary. *Woeful Afflictions: Disability and Sentimentality in Victorian America.* Philadelphia: University of Pennsylvania Press, 1999.

Kleege, Georgina. *Sight Unseen.* New Haven: Yale University Press, 1999.

Koestler, Frances. *The Unseen Minority: A Social History of Blindness in the United States.* New York: David McKay Company, 1976.

Krentz, Christopher. "A 'Vacant Receptacle'? Blind Tom, Cognitive Difference, and Pedagogy." *PMLA* 120, no. 2 (2005): 552–57.

Krieger, Nancy, and Mary Bassett. "The Health of Black Folk: Disease, Class, and Ideology in Science." In Rosenblum and Travis, *Meaning of Difference,* 393–99.

Kruth, John. *Bright Moments: The Life and Legacy of Rahsaan Roland Kirk.* New York: Welcome Rain Publishers, 2000.

Kudlick, Catherine J. "The Outlook of *The Problem* and the Problem with the *Outlook:* Two Advocacy Journals Reinvent Blind People in Turn-of-the Century America." In *New Disability History,* 187–213.

Kun, John. *Audiotopia: Music, Race, and America.* Berkeley: University of California Press, 2005.

Kunhardt Philip B., Jr., Philip B. Kuhhardt III, and Peter W. Kunhardt. *P. T. Barnum: America's Greatest Showman.* New York: Alfred A. Knopf, 1995.

Kuppers, Petra. *Disability and Contemporary Performance: Bodies on Edge.* New York: Routledge, 2003.

Lauter, Paul. "Caste, Class, and Canon." In *Feminisms: An Anthology of Literary Theory and Criticism,* ed. Robyn R. Warhol and Diane Price Herndl, 227–48. New Brunswick: Rutgers University Press, 1991.

Lee, Lawrence. "The Negro as a Problem in Public Health Charity." In Gamble, *Germs Have No Color Line,* 69–73.

Lehmann, Andreas C., and K. Anders Ericsson. "Historical Developments of Expert Performance: Public Performance of Music." In Steptoe, *Genius and the Mind,* 67–94.

Lester, James. *Too Marvelous for Words: The Life and Genius of Art Tatum.* New York: Oxford University Press, 1994.

Lester, Julius. "Country Blues Comes to Town? The View from the Other Side of the Tracks." *Sing Out!* 14, no. 4 (1964): 38.

Levine, Lawrence W. *Black Culture and Black Consciousness: Afro-American Folk Thought from Slavery to Freedom.* New York: Oxford University Press, 1977.

Lightfoot, John. "Early Texas Bluesman." In Clayton and Specht, *Roots of Texas Music,* 95–118.

Limaye, Sandhya. "Sexuality and Women with Sensory Disabilities." In Hans and Patri, *Women, Disability, and Identity,* 89–100.

Lincoln, C. Eric, and Lawrence Mamiya. "The Performed Word: Music and the

Black Church." In Abbington, *Readings in African American Church Music and Worship,* 38–75.

Linton, Simi. *Claiming Disability: Knowledge and Identity.* New York: New York University Press, 1998.

Lomax, Alan. *The Land Where the Blues Began.* New York: Pantheon Books, 1993.

Long, Lisa A. *Rehabilitating Bodies: Health, History, and the American Civil War.* Philadelphia: University of Pennsylvania Press, 2004.

Longmore, Paul K., and Lauri Umansky. "Introduction: Disability History: From the Margins to the Mainstream." In *New Disability History,* 1–29.

Lornell, Kip. "Blind Lemon Meets Leadbelly." *Black Music Research Journal* 20, no. 1 (2000): 23–33.

Lornell, Kip. *"Happy in the Service of the Lord": African-American Sacred Vocal Harmony Quartets in Memphis.* 1988. Knoxville: University of Tennessee Press, 1995.

Lornell, Kip. *Introducing American Folk Music: Ethnic and Grassroot Tradition in the United States.* 1993. New York: McGraw-Hill, 2003.

Lott, Eric. *Love and Theft: Blackface Minstrelsy and the American Working Class.* Oxford: Oxford University Press, 1993.

Love, Dennis, and Stacy Brown. *Blind Faith: The Miraculous Journey of Lula Hardaway, Stevie Wonder's Mother.* New York: Simon and Schuster, 2002.

Loveland, John. *Blessed Assurance: The Life and Hymns of Fanny J. Crosby.* Nashville: Broadman Press, 1978.

Lovell, John, Jr. *Black Song: The Forge and the Flame, The Story of How the Afro-American Spiritual Was Hammered Out.* New York: Macmillan Company, 1972.

Lowe, Allen. *American Pop from Minstrel to Mojo: On Record, 1893–1956.* Redwood, NY: Cadence Jazz Books, 1997.

Lowenfeld, Berthold. *Berthold Lowenfeld on Blindness and Blind People: Selected Papers.* New York: American Foundation for the Blind, 1981.

Lowenfeld, Berthold. *The Changing Status of the Blind: From Separation to Integration.* Springfield, IL: Charles C. Thomas Publisher, 1975.

Lowenfeld, Berthold. *Our Blind Children: Growing and Learning with Them.* Springfield, IL: Charles C. Thomas Publisher, 1964.

Lowry, Fern. "The Implications of Blindness for the Social Caseworker in Practice—Implications for the Study Process." In Finestone, *Social Casework and Blindness,* 64–86.

Lukoff, Irving F. "Attitudes toward the Blind." In Lukoff et al., *Attitudes toward Blind Persons,* 1–15.

Lukoff, Irving F. "Psychosocial Research and Severe Visual Impairment." In Graham, *Science and Blindness,* 16–24.

Lukoff, Irving F. "A Sociological Appraisal of Blindness." In Finestone, *Social Casework and Blindness,* 19–44.

Lukoff, Irving F., Oscar Cohen, et al. *Attitudes toward Blind Persons.* New York: American Foundation for the Blind, 1972.

Lukoff, Irving F., and Martin Whiteman. *The Social Sources of Adjustment to Blindness.* New York: American Foundation for the Blind, n.d.

Lydon, Michael. *Ray Charles: Man and Music.* New York: Riverhead Books, 1998.

Lykken, David T. "The Genetics of Genius." In Steptoe, *Genius and the Mind,* 15–37.

MacFarland, Douglas C. "The Blind and the Visually Impaired." In *Rehabilitation*

Practices with the Physically Disabled, ed. James F. Garrett and Edna S. Levine, 433–60. New York: Columbia University Press, 1973.

Magee, Bryan, and Martin Milligan. *On Blindness.* Oxford: Oxford University Press, 1995.

Mancuso, Chuck. *Popular Music and the Underground: Foundations of Jazz, Blues, Country, and Rock, 1900–1950.* Dubuque: Kendall/Hunt Publishing Company, 1996.

Mann, Woody. *The Anthology of Blues Guitar.* New York: Oak Publications, 1993.

Manning, Lynn. "The Magic Wand." In *Staring Back: The Disability Experience from the Inside Out,* ed. K. Fries, 165. New York: Plume, 1997.

Marks, Deborah. *Disability: Controversial Debates and Psychosocial Perspectives.* London: Routledge, 1999.

Marks, Laura U. *The Skin of the Film: Intercultural Cinema, Embodiment, and the Senses.* Durham and London: Duke University Press, 2000.

Marmor, Michael F. "The Eye and Art: Visual Function and Eye Disease in the Context of Art." In *The Eye of The Artist,* ed. Michael F. Marmor and James G. Ravin, 2–25. St. Louis: Mosby-Year Book, 1997.

Marriott, David. *On Black Men.* New York: Columbia University Press, 2000.

Martell, Joanne. *Millie-Christine: Fearfully and Wonderfully Made.* Winston-Salem: John F. Blair, Publisher, 2000.

The Marvelous Musical Prodigy, The Negro Boy Pianist Whose Recent Performances at the Great St. James and Egyptian Halls, London, and Salle Hertz, Paris, Have Created Such a Profound Sensation. Anecdotes, Songs, Sketches of the Life, Testimonials of Musical and Savans, Opinions of the American and English Press, of "Blind Tom." New York: French and Wheat, Book and Job Printers, 1867.

Mathis, Sharon Bell. *Ray Charles.* 1973. New York: Lee and Low Books, 2001.

Maultsby, Portia K. "The Impact of Gospel Music on the Secular Music Industry." In Reagon, *We'll Understand It Better By and By,* 19–33.

Maultsby, Porta K. "The Use and Performance of Hymnody, Spirituals, and Gospels in the Black Church." In Abbington, *Readings in African American Church Music and Worship,* 77–98.

Maultsby, Porta K. "West African Influences and Retentions in U.S. Black Music: A Sociocultural Study." In Jackson, *More Than Dancing,* 25–57.

McBride, David. *From TB to AIDS: Epidemics among Urban Blacks since 1900.* Albany: State University of New York Press, 1991.

McClary, Susan. *Conventional Wisdom: The Content of Musical Form.* Berkeley and Los Angeles: University of California Press, 2000.

McCoy, Eugene B. *Dr. Mattie Moss Clark; Climbing Up the Mountain: The Life and Times of a Musical Legend.* Nashville: Sparrow Press, 1994.

McGurk, Harry. "Effectance Motivation and the Development of Communicative Competence in Blind and Sighted Children." In *Language Acquisition in the Blind Child,* ed. Anne E. Mills, 108–13. London: Croom Helm, 1983.

McNamara, Brooks. *Step Right Up.* 1975. Jackson: University of Mississippi Press, 1995.

Mehta, Bejun. "A Process of Prodigy." In *Musical Prodigies: Perilous Journeys, Remarkable Lives,* ed. Claude Kenneson, 331–51. Portland, OR: Amadeus Press, 1998.

Mendl, Robert. *The Appeal of Jazz.* London: P. Allen and Co., 1927.

Merish, Lori. "Cuteness and Commodity Aesthetics: Tom Thumb and Shirley Temple." In Thomson, *Freakery*, 185–203.

Michalko, Rod. *The Difference That Disability Makes*. Philadelphia: Temple University Press, 2002.

Michalko, Rod. *The Mystery of the Eye and the Shadow of Blindness*. Toronto: University of Toronto Press, 1998.

Milian, Madeline. "Multiple Dimensions of Identity: Individuals with Visual Impairments." In Milian and Erin, *Diversity and Visual Impairment*, 35–53.

Milian, Madeline, and Jane N. Erin, eds. *Diversity and Visual Impairment: The Influence of Race, Gender, Religion, and Ethnicity on the Individual*. New York: AFB Press, 2001.

Miller, Leon K. *Musical Savants: Exceptional Skill in the Mentally Retarded*. Hillsdale, NJ: Lawrence Erlbaum Associates, 1989.

Milsap, Ronnie, and Tom Carter. *Almost like a Song*. New York: McGraw-Hill Publishing Company, 1990.

Mitchell, David T., and Sharon L. Snyder. *Narrative Prosthesis: Disability and the Dependencies of Discourse*. Ann Arbor: University of Michigan Press, 2000.

Mitchell, Gail. "Stevie Wonder: A Portrait of the Artist." *Billboard* 16, no. 50 (11 December 2004): 15–19.

Monbeck, Michael E. *The Meaning of Blindness: Attitudes toward Blindness and Blind People*. Bloomington: Indiana University Press, 1973.

Monge, Luigi. "Blindness Blues: Visual References in the Lyrics of Blind Pre-War Blues and Gospel Musicians." In *The Lyrics in American Popular Music*, ed. Robert Springer, 91–119. New York: Peter Lang, 2001.

Monge, Luigi. "The Language of Blind Lemon Jefferson: The Covert Theme of Blindness." *Black Music Research Journal* 20, no. 1 (2000): 35–69.

Moore, Allan, ed. *The Cambridge Companion to Blues and Gospel Music*. Cambridge: Cambridge University Press, 2002.

Morgan, Thomas L., and William Barlow. *From Cakewalks to Concert Halls: An Illustrated History of African American Popular Music from 1895 to 1930*. Washington, DC: Elliott and Clark Publishing, 1992.

Morgenstern, Dan. *Living with Jazz: A Reader*. Ed. Sheldon Meyer. New York: Pantheon Books, 2004.

Morse, David. *Motown*. New York: Collier Books, 1971.

Murray, Albert. *The Hero and the Blues*. 1973. New York: Vintage Books, 1995.

Murray, Albert. *Stomping the Blues*. New York: Da Capo Press, 1976.

The New Disability History: American Perspectives. New York: New York University Press, 2001. Eds. Paul K. Longmore and Lauri Umansky.

Newman, Richard. *Go Down, Moses: Celebrating the African-American Spiritual*. New York: Clarkson Potter Publishers, 1998.

Noll, Steven. *Feeble-Minded in Our Midst: Institutions for the Mentally Retarded in the South, 1900–1940*. Chapel Hill: University of North Carolina Press, 1995.

Norden, Martin F. *The Cinema of Isolation: A History of Physical Disability in the Movies*. New Brunswick: Rutgers University Press, 1994.

Oakley, Giles. *The Devil's Music: A History of the Blues*. 1976. New York: Taplinger Publishing Company, 1977.

Ochse, R. *Before the Gates of Excellence: The Determinants of Creative Genius*. Cambridge: Cambridge University Press, 1990.

Odum, Howard W., and Guy B. Johnson. *The Negro and His Songs: A Study of Typical Negro Songs in the South.* 1925. Hatboro, PA: Folklore Associates, 1964.

Oliver, Kelly. *Witnessing: Beyond Recognition.* Minneapolis: University of Minnesota Press, 2002.

Oliver, Paul. *Aspects of the Blues Tradition.* 1968. New York: Oak Publications, 1970.

Oliver, Paul. *Conversation with the Blues.* New York: Horizon Press, 1965.

Oliver, Paul. *The Meaning of the Blues.* 1960. New York: Collier Books, 1963.

Oliver, Paul. *Savannah Syncopators: African Retentions in the Blues.* New York: Stein and Day Publishers, 1970.

Oliver, Paul. *Songsters and Saints: Vocal Traditions on Race Records.* Cambridge: Cambridge University Press, 1984.

Oliver, Paul. *The Story of the Blues.* Philadelphia: Chilton Book Company, 1969.

Oliver, Paul, Max Harrison, and William Bolcolm. *The New Grove® Gospel, Blues, and Jazz with Spirituals and Ragtime.* New York: W. W. Norton and Company, 1986.

O'Neal, Jim. "I Once Was Lost but Now I'm Found: The Blues Revival of the 1960s." In Cohn, *Nothin' but the Blues,* 375–87.

Osborne, Lawrence. *American Normal: The Hidden World of Asperger Syndrome.* New York: Copernicus Books, 2002.

Oster, Harry. *Living Country Blues.* Detroit: Folklore Associates, 1969.

Palmer, Robert. *Deep Blues.* New York: Penguin Books, 1981.

Pearson, Barry. "Jump Steady: The Roots of R&B." In Cohn, *Nothin' but the Blues,* 313–47.

Peisch, Jeffrey. *Stevie Wonder.* New York: Ballantine Books, 1984.

Perone, James E. *The Sound of Stevie Wonder: His Words and Music.* Westport, CT: Praeger, 2006.

Perry, Elizabeth C., and F. Hampton Roy. *Light in the Shadows: Feelings about Blindness.* Little Rock: World Eye Foundation, 1982.

Pingree, Allison. "The 'Exceptions That Prove the Rule': Daisy and Violet Hilton, the 'New Woman,' and the Bonds of Marriage." In Thomson, *Freakery,* 173–84.

Plantinga, Leon. "The Piano and the Nineteenth Century." In Todd, *Nineteenth-Century Piano Music,* 1–15.

Pollard, C. Owen. "Agencies and Professionals Outside the Field of the Blind: Reaction." In Lukoff et al., *Attitudes toward Blind Persons,* 42–45.

Posner, Gerald. *Motown: Music, Money, Sex, and Power.* New York: Random House, 2002.

Priestly, Mark. "Disability and Old Age; or, Why It Isn't All in the Mind." In Goodley and Lawthom, *Disability and Psychology,* 84–93.

Price, Clement Alexander. "Composing the Community: Blacks Making and Teaching Music in Southern New Jersey." In *Dedicated to Music: The Legacy of African American Church Musicians and Music Teachers in Southern New Jersey, 1915–1990,* ed. Henrietta Fuller Robinson and Carolyn Cordelia Williams, xi–xxi. Cherry Hill, NJ: Africana Homestead Legacy Publishers, 1997.

Punday, Daniel. *Narrative Bodies: Toward a Corporeal Narratology.* New York: Palgrave Macmillan. 2003.

Radford, John. *Child Prodigies and Exceptional Early Achievers.* New York: Free Press, 1990.

Ramsey, Frederic, Jr., and Charles Edward Smith. *Jazzmen*. 1939. New York: Harcourt, Brace and Company, 1976.

Ramsey, Guthrie P., Jr. *Race Music: Black Cultures from Bebop to Hip-Hop*. Berkeley: University of California Press, 2003.

Reagon, Bernice Johnson. *If You Don't Go, Don't Hinder Me: The African American Sacred Song Tradition*. Lincoln: University of Nebraska Press, 2001.

Reagon, Bernice Johnson, ed. *We'll Understand It Better By and By: Pioneering African American Gospel Composers*. Washington, DC: Smithsonian Institution Press, 1992.

Reed, Teresa L. *The Holy Profane: Religion in Black Popular Music*. Lexington: University of Kentucky Press, 2003.

Reeve, Donna. "Towards a Psychology of Disability: The Emotional Effects of Living in a Disabling Society." In Goodley and Lawthom, *Disability and Psychology*, 94–108.

Reiss, Benjamin. *The Showman and the Slave: Race, Death, and Memory in Barnum's America*. Cambridge: Harvard University Press, 2001.

Richards, Graham. *"Race," Racism and Psychology: Towards Reflexive History*. London: Routledge, 1997.

Riis, Thomas L. "Blind Tom: The Legacy of a Prodigy Lost in Mystery." http://www.nytimes.com/library/music/030500ms-blind-tom.html. Accessed 20 March 2003.

Riis, Thomas L. "The Cultivated White Tradition and Black Music in Nineteenth-Century America: A Discussion of Some Articles in J. S. Dwight's Journal of Music." *Black Perspective in Music* 4, no. 2 (1976): 156–76.

Riis, Thomas L. *Just before Jazz: Black Musical Theater in New York, 1890–1915*. Washington, DC: Smithsonian Institution Press, 1989.

Ritz, David. "The Blues Is the Blood." In Guralnick et al., *Martin Scorsese Presents the Blues*, 276–78.

Roberts, Alvin. *Coping with Blindness: Personal Tales of Blindness Rehabilitation*. Carbondale: Southern Illinois University Press, 1998.

Roberts, Samuel K. *African American Christian Ethics*. Cleveland: Pilgrim Press, 2001.

Rosen, George. *The Structure of American Medical Practice, 1875–1941*. Ed. Charles E. Rosenberg. Philadelphia: University of Pennsylvania Press, 1983.

Rosenblum, Karen E., and Toni-Michelle C. Travis, eds. *The Meaning of Difference: American Constructions of Race, Sex and Gender, Social Class, and Sexual Orientation*. 1996. Boston: McGraw-Hill Higher Education, 2000.

Ross, Marlon B. *Manning the Race: Reforming Black Men in the Jim Crow Era*. New York: New York University Press, 2004.

Rouse, P. Joy. "'We Can Never Remain Silent': The Public Discourse of the Nineteenth-Century African-American Press." In *Popular Literacy: Studies in Cultural Practices and Poetics,* ed. John Trimbur, 128–42. Pittsburgh: University of Pittsburgh Press, 2001.

Ruconich, Sandra, and Katherine Standish Schneider. "Religions and Their Views of Blindness and Visual Impairment." In Milian and Erin, *Diversity and Visual Impairment*, 193–222.

Ruffin, Bernard. *Fanny Crosby*. Westwood, NJ: Barbour and Company, 1976.

Rusalem, Herbert. *Coping with the Unseen Environment: An Introduction to the Vocational Rehabilitation of Blind Persons.* New York: Teachers College Press, 1972.

Russell, Tony. *Blacks, Whites, and Blues.* New York: Stein and Day Publishers, 1970.

Russell, Tony. *The Blues: From Robert Johnson to Robert Cray.* New York: Schirmer Books, 1997.

Russell, William. "Boogie Woogie." In Ramsey and Smith, *Jazzmen,* 183–205.

Ruuth, Marianne. *Stevie Wonder.* Los Angeles: Holloway House Publishing Co., 1980.

Sackheim, Eric. *The Blues Line: A Collection of Blues Lyrics from Leadbelly to Muddy Waters.* 1969. Hopewell, NJ: Ecco Press, 1993.

Safford, Philip L., and Elizabeth J. Safford. *A History of Childhood and Disability.* New York: Teachers College Press, 1996.

Sanello, Frank. *Eddie Murphy: The Life and Times of a Comic on the Edge.* Toronto: Carol Publishing Group, 1997.

Sanjek, Russell. *American Popular Music and Its Business: The First Four Hundred Years.* Vol. 1, *The Beginning to 1790.* Oxford: Oxford University Press, 1988.

Sanjek, Russell. *American Popular Music and Its Business: The First Four Hundred Years.* Vol. 2, *From 1790 to 1909.* Oxford: Oxford University Press, 1988.

Sante, Luc. "The Blues Avant-Garde." In Guralnick et al., *Martin Scorsese Presents the Blues,* 74–75.

Santelli, Robert. *The Big Book of Blues.* New York: Penguin Books, 2001.

Santelli, Robert. "A Century of the Blues." In Guralnick et al., *Martin Scorsese Presents the Blues,* 12–59.

Santoro, Gene. *Dancing in Your Head: Jazz, Blues, Rock, and Beyond.* Oxford: Oxford University Press, 1994.

Sargeant, Winthrop. *Jazz, Hot and Hybrid.* 1938. New York: Da Capo Press, 1975.

Savitt, Todd L. *Medicine and Slavery: The Diseases and Health Care of Blacks in Antebellum Virginia.* Urbana: University of Illinois Press, 1978.

Schafer, William J., and Johannes Riedel. *The Art of Ragtime: Form and Meaning of an Original Black American Art.* Baton Rouge: Louisiana State University Press, 1973.

Schatzki, Theodore R. *The Site of the Social: A Philosophical Account of the Constitution of Social Life and Change.* University Park: Pennsylvania State University Press, 2002.

Schmidt, Barbara. *Archangels Unaware: The Story of Thomas Bethune also Known as Thomas Wiggins also Known as "Blind Tom" (1849–1908).* http://www.twain quotes.com/archangels. html. Accessed 20 March 2003.

Schon, Donald. "Research on the Blindness System(s)." In Graham, *Science and Blindness,* 98–113.

Schuller, Gunther. *Early Jazz: Its Roots and Musical Development.* New York: Oxford University Press, 1968.

Schuller, Gunther. *The Swing Era: The Development of Jazz, 1930–1945.* New York: Oxford University Press, 1989.

Schulz, Paul J. *How Does It Feel to Be Blind? The Psychodynamics of Visual Impairment.* Los Angeles: Muse-Ed Company, 1980.

Scott, Derek B. *The Singing Bourgeois: Songs of the Victorian Drawing Room and Parlour.* 1989. Aldershot: Ashgate Publishing, 2001.

Scott, Robert A. *The Making of Blind Men: A Study of Adult Socialization*. New York: Russell Sage Foundation, 1969.

Sears, Ann. "Bethune, Thomas Greene Wiggins ('Blind Tom')." In Floyd, *International Dictionary of Black Composers, Volume 1*, 105–8.

Sears, Ann. "Boone, John William ('Blind Boone')." In Floyd, *International Dictionary of Black Composers: Volume 1*, 138–42.

Sears, Ann. "John William 'Blind' Boone, Pianist-Composer: 'Merit, Not Sympathy Wins.'" *Black Music Research Journal* 9, no. 2 (1989): 225–47.

Shaw, Arnold. *Honkers and Shouters: The Golden Years of Rhythm and Blues*. New York: Macmillan Publishing Co., 1978.

Shaw, Arnold. *The World of Soul: Black America's Contribution to the Pop Music Scene*. New York: Cowles Book Company, 1970.

Shearing, George, and Alyn Shipton. *Lullaby of Birdland: The Autobiography of George Shearing*. New York: Continuum, 2004.

Shelly, Susan, et al., eds. *The Encyclopedia of Blindness and Vision Impairment*. 2nd ed. New York: Facts on File, 2002.

Shepherd, John, and Peter Wicke. *Music and Cultural Theory*. Cambridge: Polity Press, 1997.

Silvers, Anita, David Wasserman, and Mary B. Mahowald. *Disability, Difference, Discrimination: Perspectives on Justice in Bioethics and Public Policy*. Lanham, MD: Rowman and Littlefield Publishers, 1998.

Sizer, Lyde Cullen. *The Political Work of Northern Women Writers and the Civil War, 1850–1872*. Chapel Hill: University of North Carolina Press, 2000.

Smart, Julie. *Disability, Society, and the Individual*. Gaithersburg, MD: Aspen Publications, 2001.

Smith, Charles Edward. "White New Orleans." In Ramsey and Smith, *Jazzmen*, 39–58.

Smith, Jane Stuart, and Betty Carson. *Favorite Women Hymn Writers*. Wheaton, IL: Crossway Books, 1990.

Southall, Geneva H. *Blind Tom, the Black Pianist-Composer (1849–1908): Continually Enslaved*. Lanhan, MD: Scarecrow Press, 1999.

Southall, Geneva H. *Blind Tom: The Post–Civil War Enslavement of a Black Musical Genius: Book I*. Minneapolis: Challenge Productions, 1979.

Southall, Geneva H. *The Continuing Enslavement of Blind Tom: The Black Pianist-Composer (1865–1887): Book II*. Minneapolis: Challenge Productions, 1983

Southern, Eileen. "Hymnals of the Black Church." In Abbington, *Readings in African American Church Music and Worship*, 137–51.

Southern, Eileen. *The Music of Black Americans: A History*. 1971. 3rd ed. New York: W. W. Norton and Company, 1997.

Spencer, Frederick J. *Jazz and Death: Medical Profiles of Jazz Greats*. Jackson: University of Mississippi Press, 2002.

Spencer, Jon Michael. *Black Hymnody: A Hymnological History of the African-American Church*. Knoxville: University of Tennessee Press, 1992.

Spencer, Jon Michael. *Blues and Evil*. Knoxville: University of Tennessee Press, 1993.

Spencer, Jon Michael. *Re-Searching Black Music*. Knoxville: University of Tennessee Press, 1996

Springer, Robert. *Authentic Blues: Its History and Its Themes.* 1985. Trans. André J. M. Prévos and Robert Springer. Lewiston, NY: Edwin Mellen Press, 1995.

Stadler, Gustavus. *Troubling Minds: The Cultural Politics of Genius in the United States, 1840–1890.* Minneapolis: University of Minnesota Press, 2006.

Starr, S. Frederick. *Bamboula! The Life and Times of Louis Moreau Gottschalk.* Oxford: Oxford University Press, 1995.

Stearns, Marshall. *The Story of Jazz.* London: Oxford University Press, 1958.

Steptoe, Andrew, ed. *Genius and the Mind: Studies of Creativity and Temperament.* Oxford: Oxford University Press, 1998.

Stewart, Rex. *Jazz Masters of the 30s.* New York: Da Capo Press, 1972.

Stiker, Henri-Jacques. *A History of Disability.* 1997. Trans. William Sayers. Ann Arbor: University of Michigan Press, 1999.

Stivale, Charles J. *Disenchanting Les Bon Temps: Identity and Authenticity in Cajun Music and Dance.* Durham: Duke University Press, 2003.

Stock, Jonathan P. J. *Musical Creativity in Twentieth-Century China: Abing, His Music, and Its Changing Meanings.* Rochester: University of Rochester Press, 1996.

Sweet, Leonard I. *Health and Medicine in the Evangelical Tradition: "Not By Might Nor Power."* Valley Forge: Trinity Press International, 1994.

Swenson, John. *Stevie Wonder.* New York: Harper and Row, Publishers, 1986.

"The Tale of 'Blind Tom' Wiggins." 20 March 2003. http://www.npr.org/programs/morning/features/2002/mar/blindtom/index.html. Accessed 20 March 2003.

Taylor, Billy. *Jazz Piano: A Jazz History.* Dubuque: Wm. C. Brown Company Publishers, 1983.

tenBroek, Jacobus, and Floyd. W. Matson. *Hope Deferred: Public Welfare and the Blind.* Berkeley: University of California Press, 1959.

"Thomas Greene Bethune." 20 March 2003. http://docsouth.unc.edu/neh/bethune/bethune.html. Accessed 20 March 2003.

Thomson, Rosemarie Garland. "The Beauty and the Freak." In *Points of Contact: Disability, Art, and Culture,* ed. Susan Crutchfield and Marcy Epstein, 181–96. Ann Arbor: University of Michigan Press, 2000.

Thomson, Rosemarie Garland. *Extraordinary Bodies: Figuring Physical Disability in American Culture and Literature.* New York: Columbia University Press, 1997.

Thomson, Rosemarie Garland, ed. *Freakery: Cultural Spectacles of the Extraordinary Body.* New York: New York University Press, 2003.

Thomson, Rosemarie Garland. "Introduction: From Wonder to Error—A Genealogy of Freak Discourse in Modernity." In Thomson, *Freakery,* 1—19.

Thomson, Rosemarie Garland. "Narrative of Deviance and Delight: Staring at Julia Pastrana, the 'Extraordinary Lady.'" In *Beyond the Binary: Reconstructing Cultural Identity in a Multicultural Context,* ed. Timothy Powell, 81–104. New Brunswick: Rutgers University Press, 1999.

Thomson, Rosemarie Garland. "Seeing the Disabled: Visual Rhetorics of Disability in Popular Photography." In *New Disability History,* 335–75.

Thurman, Howard. *Deep River and The Negro Spiritual Speaks of Life and Death.* Richmond, IN: Friends United Press, 1975.

Tilling, Robert, ed. *Oh, What a Beautiful City: A Tribute to the Reverend Gary Davis (1896–1972).* Jersey, UK: Paul Mill Press, 1992.

Tirro, Frank. *Jazz: A History.* 1977. 2nd ed. New York: W. W. Norton and Company, 1993.

Titchkosky, Tanya. *Disability, Self, and Society.* Toronto: University of Toronto Press, 2003.

Titon, Jeff Todd *Early Downhome Blues: A Musical and Cultural Analysis.* Chicago: University of Illinois Press, 1977.

Todd, R. Larry, ed. *Nineteenth-Century Piano Music.* New York: Schirmer Books, 1990.

Tolbert, Odie H. "A Brief Overview of African-American Gospel Music." In *African-American Good News (Gospel) Music,* by Sherry Sherrod Dupree and Herbert C. Dupree, vi. Washington, DC: Middle Atlantic Regional Press, 1993.

Tosches, Nick. *Where Dead Voices Gather.* Boston: Little Brown and Company, 2001.

Touma, Habib Hassan. *The Music of the Arabs.* Portland, OR: Amadeus Press, 1996.

Treffert, Darold. *Extraordinary People: Understanding "Idiot Savants."* New York: Harper and Row, 1989.

Trevor-Roper, Patrick . *The World through Blunted Sight: An Inquiry into the Influence of Defective Vision on Art and Character.* London: Allen Lane, Penguin Press, 1988.

Trotter, James M. *Music and Some Highly Musical People.* 1881. New York: Johnson Reprint Corporation, 1968.

Turk, Ruth. *Ray Charles: Soul Man.* Minneapolis: Lerner Publications Company, 1996.

Turner, Bryan S. *The Body and Society: Explorations in Social Theory.* New York: Basil Blackwell, 1984.

Tuttle, Dean W., and Naomi R. Tuttle. *Self-Esteem and Adjusting with Blindness: The Process of Responding to Life's Demands.* Springfield, IL: Charles C. Thomas Publisher, 1996.

Twain, Mark. "Blind Tom." http://twainquotes.com/18690801.html. Accessed 20 March 2003.

Uzzel, Robert L. *Blind Lemon Jefferson: His Life, His Death, and His Legacy.* Austin: Eakin Press, 2002.

Vaughan, C. Edwin. *The Struggle of Blind People for Self-Determination: The Dependency-Rehabilitation Conflict: Empowerment in the Blindness Community.* Springfield, IL: Charles C. Thomas Publisher, 1993,

Waldo, Terry. *This Is Ragtime.* New York: Hawthorn Books, 1976.

Walker, Wyatt Tee. *"Somebody's Calling My Name": Black Sacred Music and Social Change.* 1979. Valley Forge: Judson Press, 1992.

Walser, Robert. "Deep Jazz: Notes on Interiority, Race, and Criticism." In *Inventing the Psychological: Toward a Cultural History of Emotional Life in America,* ed. Joel Pfister and Nancy Schnog, 271–96. New Haven: Yale University Press, 1997.

Walton, Ortiz M. *Music: Black, White, and Blue.* New York: William Morrow and Company, 1972.

Ward, Andrew. *Dark Midnight When I Rise: The Story of the Jubilee Singers Who Introduced the World to the Music of Black America.* New York: Farrar, Straus, and Giroux, 2000.

Ward, Brian. *Just My Soul Responding: Rhythm and Blues, Black Consciousness, and Race Relations.* Berkeley and Los Angeles: University of California Press, 1998.

Warren, Gwendolin Sims. *Ev'ry Time I Feel the Spirit: 101 Best-Loved Psalms, Gospel Hymns, and Spiritual Songs of the African-American Church.* New York: Henry Holt and Company, 1997.

Watley, William D. "The Tradition of Worship." In Abbington, *Readings in African American Church Music and Worship,* 81–295.

Watterson, Henry. "Henry Watterson's Memories of Blind Tom." *Courier-Journal,* 16 June 1908. http://www.twainquotes.com/watterson-trib.html. Accessed 20 March 2003.

Welding, Pete. "The Birth of the Blues." In *The Guitar: The History, the Music, the Players,* ed. Gene Santoro, 51–89. New York: William Morrow and Company, 1984.

Welding, Pete, and Toby Byron, eds. *Bluesland: Portraits of Twelve Major American Blues Masters.* New York: Dutton, 1991.

Wendell, Susan. *The Rejected Body: Feminist Philosophical Reflections on Disability.* New York: Routledge, 1996.

Wenders, Wim. "The Soul of a Man." In Guralnick et al., *Martin Scorsese Presents the Blues,* 156–64.

Werner, Craig. *Higher Ground: Stevie Wonder, Aretha Franklin, Curtis Mayfield, and the Rise and Fall of American Soul.* New York: Crown Publishers, 2004.

White, Timothy. *Rock Lives: Profiles and Interviews.* New York: Henry Holt and Company, 1990.

Wilds, Mary. *Raggin' the Blues: Legendary Country Blues and Ragtime Musicians.* Greensboro, NC: Avisson Press, 2001.

Williams, Martin. *Jazz Masters In Transition, 1957–69.* 1970. New York: Da Capo Press, 1982.

Williams, Tenley. *Stevie Wonder.* Philadelphia: Chelsea House Publishers, 2002.

Williams-Jones, Pearl. "Roberta Martin: Spirit of an Era." In Reagon, *We'll Understand It Better By and By,* 255–74.

Wilson, James C., and Cynthia Lewiecki-Wilson. "Disability, Rhetoric, and the Body." In Wilson and Lewiecki-Wilson, *Embodied Rhetorics,* 1–24.

Wilson, James C., and Cynthia Lewiecki-Wilson, eds. *Embodied Rhetorics: Disability in Language and Culture.* Carbondale: Southern Illinois University Press, 2001.

Winan, Robert B. "Early Minstrel Show Music, 1843–1852." In *Inside the Minstrel Mask: Readings in Nineteenth-Century Blackface Minstrelsy,* ed. Annemarie Bean, James V. Hatch, and Brooks McNamara, 141–62. Hanover: Wesleyan University Press, 1996.

Winski, Norman. *Ray Charles: Singer and Musician.* Los Angeles: Melrose Square Publishing Company, 1994.

Winter, Robert S. "Orthodoxies, Paradoxes, and Contradictions: Performance Practices in Nineteenth-Century Piano Music." In Todd, *Nineteenth-Century Piano Music,* 16–54.

Witek, Joseph. "Blindness as a Rhetorical Trope in Blues Discourse." *Black Music Research Journal* 8, no. 2 (1988): 35–69, 177–93.

Wolfe, Charles K. *Kentucky Country: Folk and Country Music of Kentucky.* Lexington: University Press of Kentucky, 1982.

Wolfe, Charles, and Kip Lornell. *The Life and Legend of Leadbelly.* New York: HarperCollins Publishers, 1992.

Woodfin, Henry. "Ray Charles." In *Jazz Panorama: From the Pages of* The Jazz Review, ed. Martin T. Williams, 306–10. 1962. New York: Da Capo Press, 1979.

Woods, Clyde. *Development Arrested: The Blues and Plantation Power in the Mississippi Delta.* London: Verso, 1998.

Wrigley, Owen. *The Politics of Deafness.* Washington, DC: Gallaudet University Press, 1996.

Wynter, Leon E. *American Skin: Pop Culture, Big Business, and the End of White America.* New York: Crown Publishers, 2002.

York, Adrian. "Keyboard Technique." In Moore, *Cambridge Companion to Blues and Gospel Music,* 130–40.

Young, Alan. *The Pilgrim Jubilees.* Jackson: University Press of Mississippi, 2001.

Young, Alan. *Woke Me Up This Morning: Black Gospel Singers and the Gospel Life.* Jackson: University Press of Mississippi, 1997.

Young, Iris Marion. *Justice and the Politics of Difference.* Princeton: Princeton University Press, 1990.

Yuan, David D. "The Celebrity Freak: Michael Jackson's 'Grotesque Glory.'" In Thomson, *Freakery,* 368–84.

Zolten, Jerry. *Great God A' Mighty! The Dixie Hummingbirds: Celebrating the Rise of Soul Gospel Music.* New York: Oxford University Press, 2003.

Index